D0098015

JEREMIAH
and
LAMENTATIONS

JEREMIAH
and
LAMENTATIONS

by
IRVING L. JENSEN

moody press
chicago

To

Our Children,
Donna, Karen, Bobby

Jeremiah

Copyright ©, 1966, by
THE MOODY BIBLE INSTITUTE
OF CHICAGO

Lamentations

© 1974 by
THE MOODY BIBLE INSTITUTE
OF CHICAGO

Second Printing, 1976

ISBN: 0-8024-2024-9

Printed in the United States of America

CONTENTS

3

PREFACE

JEREMIAH is one of the five books of the Major Prophets, which are called "major" primarily from the standpoint of the length of the prophecies. (The book of Lamentations is very short, but it is part of this group of five because it is like an appendix to Jeremiah's prophecy.) The shorter prophetical books, known as the Minor Prophets, are no less important; but, at the same time, one cannot escape the divine intention of emphasis by the repetition and amplification so evident in the long messages of the Major Prophets. The message of Jeremiah is vital, and it is the writer's hope that this brief commentary will give a clearer understanding of that message in order that the reader may apply it to his own life.

As in his commentary on Numbers, the writer has used the American Standard Version for the basic biblical text. The reader using the King James Version in connection with this study will not, however, be at any disadvantage. Whatever version is used, it is important for the student of Jeremiah to proceed paragraph by paragraph in the biblical text, rather than verse by verse, to get the thrust of the larger units of thought. This commentary attempts to help the reader in such a paragraphical study.

It is important in Bible study always to read the portion of the biblical text before reading any commentary on it. The commentary then is seen to be more pertinent and directional, while the Bible becomes more quickening and fruitful.

May the study of this faithful prophet of God challenge the reader to a courageous stand on the foundations of the DIVINE WORD, and lead to deeper insights into the fathomless truths of GOD'S SOVEREIGNTY.

—IRVING L. JENSEN

INTRODUCTION

JUST AS THE DESTRUCTION of Jerusalem in A.D. 70 with the subsequent worldwide dispersion of the Jews was a climax of judgment for the Jews' rejection of the Messiah, so the fall of the holy city in 586 B.C. with the associated captivity of Judah in a foreign land was the catastrophic judgment of God's chosen people in Old Testament days. Less than a hundred years later a remnant of the exiles returned and the city and temple were rebuilt, but the splendor and glory of Mt. Zion had faded away. Only a new day in the millennial age would see that splendor again. If in the history of God's people in Old Testament days the fall of Jerusalem in 586 B.C. was *the* crucial and pivotal event, then the Prophet Jeremiah, who was about sixty-five when the city fell, was its key person.

The sixth-century B.C. books of Jeremiah are important for the twentieth-century world because the similarities between Jeremiah's day and today could hardly be stronger: today is a time of deep sin, as then; apostasy and hypocrisy abound today, as then; the balance of power among nations totters precariously and alliances change with apparent recklessness from decade to decade; God's heralds are in a lonely minority; and the rumblings of doomsday, like an approaching avalanche, get louder by the minute. Very evident in the message of Jeremiah is the fact that the destinies of peoples and nations are not fulfilled outside the hand of God. During these last days of the Church on earth, the Christian will find in these ancient books a timely message and many answers to questions about the ways of God in the world today and to-morrow.

Characteristics of the Book of Jeremiah

Unlike the book of Isaiah, which contains comparatively little of the life of its author, Jeremiah has much in it that is autobiographical and confessional. (See his confessions in 10:23-24; 11:18—12:6; 15:10-18; 17:9-11, 14-18; 18:18-23; 20:7-18.) One of the obvious intentions of God in the prophecy is to reveal the tremendous cost of being one of His prophets to an apostate people and to heathen nations, with all the pressures, persecutions, problems, and passions involved.[1] The book teaches other major truths, but this insight into the cost of proclaiming God's truth is one of the book's priceless teachings for the servant of God.

The prophecy of Jeremiah is basically composed of discourses (or oracles), with narrative portions interspersed throughout. They appear in the pattern of the following sequence: chapters 1 through 20, mainly prophetic oracles; 21 through 33, an interweaving of discourse and narrative; 34 through 45, mainly narrative; 46 through 52, mainly oracles. The oracles spoken to men or nations are usually introduced with the authoritative "Thus saith the Lord" or its equivalent, and are composed in a style that reflects Hebrew poetry.[2]

[1]Lamentations, traditionally thought to have been written by Jeremiah, vividly portrays the prophet's passion of sorrow over the destruction of the holy city, Jerusalem.

[2]E.g., see the poetic format in *The Westminster Study Edition of the Holy Bible* (Philadelphia: Westminster Press), in Harold Lindsell (ed.), *Harper Study Bible* (New York: Harper & Row, 1964), and in Philip Schaff (ed.), "Jeremiah," *Lange's Commentary on the Holy Scriptures,* Vol. 6 (Grand Rapids: Zondervan Pub. House, n.d.).

Another characteristic of the book of Jeremiah is the nonchronological order of its parts. In one's first survey of the book as a whole, this becomes a disturbing or at least confusing observation. But the fact of a nonchronological sequence indicates to the student that wherever chronology was sacrificed, the purpose was to furnish a topical study of the subject at hand. Actually, when the entire book is broken down into large divisions, and chronology is sought in each such division, a substratum of general chronology is seen to underlie those sections of the book. Such a breakdown reveals: chapters 1 through 20, generally chronological; 21 through 44, chronological with the exception of the insertion of material at two locations; 45 through 52, chronological. (See Appendix I for the scheme of Jeremiah's chronology.)

Broad Survey of Jeremiah

Jeremiah is one of the five books of the Major Prophets, the classification *major* referring to the long length of these books. Jeremiah contains fifty-two chapters, second in length to Isaiah's sixty-six.

On a first cursory reading of the entire book, where general impressions are sought, the student cannot help but observe the following: (1) the atmosphere is one of warning and doom, (2) there is a progression to a climax in the destruction of Jerusalem (chap. 39), (3) seeds of hope are scattered here and there, and (4) there appears to be a disconnectedness about some of the parts. This latter observation is a challenge to study the flow of the book more closely by first identifying groups of materials. In such a study the following groupings stand out boldly: the commissioning of Jeremiah, chapter 1; a series of prophecies of doom, 2 through 20; Nebuchadnezzar-related chapters, 21 through 29; the new covenant, 30 through 33; the siege and fall of Jerusalem, 34 through 39; Jeremiah's experiences after the the fall of Jerusalem, 40 through 44; oracles concerning foreign nations, 46 through 51; and another section on the fall of Jerusalem, 52. These groupings, when related to the crucial event of the book, Jerusalem's fall, crystallize into an overall pattern of the book, as indicated by the following outline:

Jeremiah's call is a fitting introduction to the book (chap. 1). This is followed by the division "Discourses," which, together with chapter 1, may be called Book I (see Appendix I). This division contains the substance of Jeremiah's preaching against sin and warning of judgment to come. Chapters 11 through 20 relate some of the personal experiences of the prophet in which the message of Jehovah to the people was made very vivid and real, first to Jeremiah, and then to the people (e.g., the linen girdle episode, chap. 13).

Book II (21-44) begins with specific prophecies of the inevitable destruction of Jerusalem, the name Nebuchadnezzar[3] first appearing in 21:2. The climax of this division, the fall of Jerusalem itself, is reached in chapter 39 of the narrative section, after which an accounting of the effects of and sequels to the fall is made (40-44).

Chapter 44 ends the main body of the prophecy of Jeremiah. Chapters 45 through 52 may be considered a series of supplementary sections. Chapter 45 gives light about the reaction of Jeremiah's scribe, Baruch, to his task.

---

[3]The names Nebudchadnezzar and Nebudchadrezzar are the Jewish and Babylonian spellings, respectively, of the same name. The Akkadian form, Nabukudurri-usur, literally means "Nabu, protect my boundary."

BOOK I		BOOK II				SUPPLEMENTS		
DISCOURSES		SPECIAL PROPHECIES		NARRATIVE				
2 Public Sermons	11 Personal Experiences	21 Certainty of Captivity	30 Hope of Salvation	34 Siege and Fall of Jerusalem	40 After Fall	45 BARUCH	46 Foreign Nations	52 Fall of Jerusalem

INTRO — CALL

FALL (at Siege and Fall of Jerusalem) — FALL (at Fall of Jerusalem, ch. 52)

Scale: 1 — 11 — 21 — 45 — 52

Chapters 46 through 51 amplify what was given in chapter 25 concerning the future destinies of the surrounding nations. Chapter 52 retells the events of Jerusalem's fall.

Historical Background

Kings of Judah During Jeremiah's Ministry. The Northern Kingdom of Israel was taken into captivity in 722 B.C., about one hundred years before Jeremiah began to preach to Judah. At that time Ahaz was the king of Judah, the Southern Kingdom. Subsequently Judah's throne passed in succession to: Hezekiah (715-686),[4] a good king; Manasseh (695-642), whose reign has been described as a political whirlpool and moral cesspool; Amon (642-640); Josiah (640-609), who instituted a program of religious reform, much of which was only external; Jehoahaz (Shallum) (609), who was deposed by Neco, king of Egypt; Jehoiakim (609-597), who ruled despotically as a puppet of Egypt; Jehoiachin (597); and Zedekiah (597-586), whose vacillating reign came to an end with the fall of Jerusalem. See Appendix II for further description and identification of the above-named kings.

According to 1:2-3, Jeremiah began his prophetic ministry in the thirteenth year of Josiah's reign (627), and continued through the critical reigns of Jehoiakim and Zedekiah into the captivity period.

Leading Foreign Nations During Jeremiah's Ministry. When Jeremiah's ministry began, Judah was subject to Assyria,[5] then a world power for almost three hundred

---

[4]Note that Hezekiah and Manasseh ruled as coregents for several years. Most of the dates of this commentary are those given by John C. Whitcomb in his chart "Old Testament Kings and Prophets," Grace Theological Seminary, Winona Lake, Indiana.

[5]Acquaintance with the geography of the book is important for the student of Jeremiah. See Appendix III for the related map.

years. When the Assyrian capital, Nineveh, fell in 612, Assyrian dominance vaporized; Egypt and Babylon vied for the suzerainty. The Battle of Carchemish (605) decided the issue, leaving Babylon[6] as *the* power. Judah was then subject to Babylon. But after 605 Egypt was successful, on occasions, in making overtures to Judah's kings, hoping that the secret alliances would eventually favor Egypt's chances of one day conquering Babylon.

Part of Jeremiah's task was to convince the people and rulers of Judah that Babylon, the nation from the "north" (4:6), was the divinely destined master of Judah for the near future, and that Judah's flirting relations with other nations would add to the horror of the doom to come. But his appeals were rejected. In 588 the Babylonian conqueror, Nebuchadnezzar, did come, the siege of Jerusalem began, and about thirty months later (586) the city and its temple were utterly destroyed.

See Appendix II for a chronological chart identifying the times of Jeremiah's ministry, the kings of Judah, the world powers, Neo-Babylonian kings, and the Egyptian kings.

The Man Jeremiah

There was apparently nothing auspicious about the career of Jeremiah in his early years as priest in the small town of Anathoth. Then, as though out of nowhere, God reached down and marked the priest to be His prophet,

---

[6]The name "Neo-Babylonian Empire" which refers to the empire of the geographical Babylon of Jeremiah's time, extended in time from the beginning of the reign of Nabopolassar (626 B.C.) to the fall of Babylon (539 B.C.). In area the empire included Babylonia, Assyria, Syria, Phoenicia, and Palestine. The name "Chaldeans" is synonymous with "Neo-Babylonians." Any reference in this commentary to Babylonians is in effect a reference to the Chaldeans or Neo-Babylonians.

launching him on a special mission that would engage him for the rest of his life.

God knew whom He was calling (1:5). Whatever were the noble spiritual qualities of Jeremiah at the time of the divine call to be a prophet, there was an abundance of them manifested consistently during his career. He had a keen awareness that God was real; his faith was dauntless; he believed in prayer; he was willing to suffer for God's sake. Jeremiah was by nature gentle and meek, patient and brave, candid and passionate. His honesty would not let him be bribed; his deep emotions would not give place to a stony resignation to judgment. He was utterly devoted to one task, that of preaching the message of God. As someone has put it, he was the "bravest, grandest man of Old Testament history."

The Theme of the Prophecy

The theme of Jeremiah's prophecy may be stated thus: A prophet's voice for the sovereign judgments of God. Three main subjects are involved:

The prophet: The story of the man of God and the fulfillment of his mission as a voice for God is woven throughout the prophecy in both narrative and discourse sections.

The sovereignty of God: From the first chapter to the last, God calls the signals and brings the events to pass.

Judgment: Much is learned of grace and mercy in the book (e.g., God's long-suffering, and the restoration and covenant promises), but the major thrust of the book is that of God's judgments on sin.

Purposes of the Commentary

In order to faithfully represent the contents of this extensive prophetic work in a brief study guide, attention can be devoted only to the primary and grand truths of the books. Many details of necessity must remain unrecorded; some details are crucial; all the details must be recognized in their rightful place.

The writer has attempted to furnish the student with (1) a guide to the background of the writings, (2) an overall survey of the contents of the books, showing the basic unity in what they teach, (3) analytical studies of the main subjects of the prophecy, and (4) an incentive to apply the many spiritual lessons of the books to Christian living and the world today.

JEREMIAH

BOOK ONE

3. The Drought: Jeremiah As the Interceding Priest (14:1-22)
4. From Despondency to Hope: Jeremiah As the Rejected Intercessor (15:1-21)
5. In This Place: Jeremiah Alone in a Punished Place (16:1-18)
6. The Heart: Jeremiah Remains True in Heart (16:19—17:18)
7. The Law of the Sabbath: Jeremiah Preaches at the City's Gates (17:19-27)
8. Lessons from Pottery: Jeremiah Learns and Preaches from Pottery (18:1—20:18)

I. INTRODUCTION (1:1-19)

NO MORE FITTING INTRODUCTION to the prophecy of Jeremiah could be given in the opening words of the prophecy than by stating where God "found" Jeremiah (among the priests), and what He made of him (a prophet unto the nations).

A. Jeremiah, Priest of Anathoth (1:1-3)

Anathoth, a town about three miles northeast of Jerusalem, was assigned to and inhabited by priests (Joshua 21:13-19; I Chron. 6:57-60). Here Jeremiah was born, son of the priest Hilkiah. The name his parents gave him literally meant "Jah is high," or "whom Jah appoints." Jeremiah was evidently a very young man when, in the thirteenth year of Josiah's reign (627 B.C.), he was called to be a prophetic word-bearer for God. That ministry was to continue during the reigns of the two major kings succeeding Josiah, namely, Jehoiakim and Zedekiah, "unto the carrying away of Jerusalem captive" (1:3).

18

B. Jeremiah, Prophet unto the Nations (1:4-19)

The formal introduction has been given. (Most of the chapters in the book are introduced in the style of a reporter's writing, with the formal third person, in phrases such as "The word that came to Jeremiah from Jehovah," 7:1.) Now Jeremiah begins to write in the testimonial first person, "Now the word of Jehovah came unto *me*" (1:4). Here, at the time of his appointment, when God has called him from the priesthood and has commissioned him to be a prophet, Jeremiah's autobiographical style points up the emotional experience of a critical day in his life.

1. *Sovereign Appointment* (1:4-10)

Far more important than learning what task he must accomplish, Jeremiah needed to know with assurance the person who was commissioning him. God identified Himself to be sovereign over Jeremiah in that He (1) foreknew Jeremiah before he was born, (2) had caused him to be born, and (3) had separated him for a holy service. On this basis, He also had the sovereign prerogative to appoint Jeremiah to be a prophet. Could Jeremiah avoid this moment of truth upon which his future career depended?

Jeremiah did try to shrink from the appointment, not because of a selfish motive but because he felt incompetent. His record relates that he heaved a deep sigh to God, "Ah!" expressing his feeling that he did not have the know-how. His "I am a child" perhaps revealed his brief experience as well as his comparatively young age.[1] But God

---

[1] The Hebrew word for child, *na'ar,* could refer to any age up to about forty-five. (Joshua was a *na'ar* at forty-five: Exodus 33:11.) It is generally believed that Jeremiah was between twenty and twenty-five when this call came to him.

objected that he was looking at himself and taking his eyes off his sovereign Master. "Say not, *I* [Jeremiah] . . . ," God rebuked Jeremiah. "*I* [God] shall send thee . . . *I* shall command thee . . . *I* am with thee . . . *I* have put *my* words in thy mouth . . . *I* have this day set thee over. . . ." (1:7-10). God's words in Jeremiah's mouth were to be mostly words of doom and death ("pluck up, break down, destroy, overthrow"), but they would also be words of hope, and life ("build, plant"), such as the consolation messages of chapters 31 through 33. Jeremiah was to pluck up dead ritual and plant living worship, pluck up vile ways and plant straight paths, pluck up degenerate hearts and plant new hearts of a new covenant. Such were the involvements of Jeremiah's sovereign appointment.

2. *Sovereign Word* (1:11-16)

Next it was necessary for Jeremiah to get a true perspective of words, to distinguish between God's words and man's words. God has just spoken to Jeremiah of *"my* words in *thy* mouth" (1:9). Jeremiah was to be the mere channel; God's words were the product to be delivered. To illustrate to Jeremiah the sovereign nature of the words or the will of God, Jeremiah was given his first two prophetic visions at this time. The vision experience, which would be rather frequent during his prophetic ministry, was given by God for durable impression.

The Almond (Awake) Tree (1:11-12). Jeremiah saw in the first vision a shoot or twig of an almond tree. "Almond tree" is the translation of the Hebrew word *shaqed* which literally means "awake." "Thou hast seen well," said God, "for I *watch over* [Hebrew word for 'watch' is *shoqed*] my word to perform it." The connection of the vision and the application may be seen in the fact that the almond tree, blossoming around January, was the first tree to awaken from the long winter's night, its blossoms appearing before the leaves. The symbol of awakeness befitted God's Word, for though His people had settled into a dark, cold sleep of spiritual dearth, His Word was ever awake, watched over by Him, bringing about its daily unalterable fulfillment of sovereign design.

The Boiling Caldron (1:13-16). This vision was given Jeremiah to reveal the main forthcoming event of the performance (awakeness) of God's Word, in the life of Israel. One specific of that Word was the inevitable judgment for sin. The sin of God's people is described here as desertion and idolatry (1:16). For this wickedness the seething, scorching judgment of God would be poured out on the people, "out of the north." At the time of this vision Assyria, not Babylon, was the great world empire, but God was prophetically referring to the Babylonians, as can be seen from (1) Jeremiah's specific reference to Babylon and the North as recorded in 25:9, and (2) the actual fulfillment of the prophecy in the taking of Jerusalem by the Chaldeans, in 586 (chap. 39). Although Babylon was located geographically due east of Judah, her invading armies would have to come upon Jerusalem from the North, because of the impassable Arabian Desert.

3. *Sovereign Protection* (1:17-19)

Compared to Jeremiah's original fears when God earlier commissioned him to be a prophet, his apprehensions by now must have grown intense. Scalding, boiling judgment from the North! And this is the word Jeremiah must speak to his people. "Thou therefore gird up thy loins, and arise, and speak unto them" (1:17). Jeremiah doesn't record his feelings at this point, but they are implied by God's antici-

21

patory "be not dismayed at them" (1:17). On what basis could Jeremiah dispel his fears? On this, that even as he could anchor his life to the design of God's *sovereign appointment* and the inevitable fulfillment of God's *sovereign Word,* so now he may rest in the assurance of God's *sovereign protection.* "As of now," said God, "I have made you a fortified city — impregnable, unassailable — against the onslaughts of kings, princes, priests, and people. They shall fight but not prevail, 'for I am with thee, to deliver thee' " (1:18-19). Jeremiah would be famous but not popular, for who loves a pessimist! However, his triumph was to be "not his fame, but his faithfulness."[2]

* * *

Thus Jeremiah was thrust into the role of word-bearer for God, to be unpopular and hated by men, but loved and protected by his sovereign Lord. Who of us would tread that path?

II. DISCOURSES (2:1—20:18)

A. Public Sermons (2:1—10:25)

Jeremiah, appointed to the mixed task of declaring denunciation, visitation, invitation, and consolation, reported for active duty. The first order of the day was to preach public sermons to the populace: "Go, and cry in the ears of Jerusalem" (2:2). Chapters 2 through 10 record those sermons. Some were delivered in the temple, others, apparently, on the street corner.

1. *Backsliding Israel* (2:1-37)[3]

----

[2]Fred M. Wood, *Fire in My Bones* (Nashville: *Broadman Press,* 1959), p. 24.

[3]It is recommended that in the study of each of the sermons of Jeremiah the *paragraph divisions* be recognized as identifying units of thought within each segment of the sermon. A suggested set of paragraph divisions for each of the segments of Book I is given

There is a just reason for every judgment of God. Before the first wall of the holy city would totter from the ceaseless batterings of the enemy, its people (*God's* people! 2:11,32) would be told every reason for the oncoming woeful tragedy; their sins would be spelled out very clearly, from the God-touched lips of Jeremiah. This, Jeremiah's first recorded public sermon, did just that for the people. Its theme: "Thy backslidings [literally, 'turnings back'] shall reprove thee" (2:19).

The message had three parts. The first (2:1-8) compared Israel's past and the present. In the middle section (2:9-25), God asked, in effect, "Why have my people chosen the bad?" The last section (2:26-37) foretold the future.

a. An Unfaithful Wife (God's remorse over rejected love, 2:1-8). Using the intimate figure of love and marriage, God recalls Israel's[4] first tender love toward Him, the kindness of her youth, and how she followed after Him as His own in the wilderness (2:2). Those were days when the people were a holy witness unto the Lord and manifested to others His quickening power in their lives to produce the most precious fruit, eternal fruit (2:3a).

But now! It is tragic that Jeremiah's generation had not gone the way of their fathers; they who had once

the reader in the footnotes. For this sermon, make paragraph divisions at verses 1, 4, 9, 14, 20, 26, 29. For practical suggestions on a paragraphical method of Bible study, see Irving L. Jensen, *Independent Bible Study* (Chicago: Moody Press, 1963), pages 116 ff.

[4]The terms "Judah" and "Israel" are used for the most part interchangeably in Jeremiah, Judah appearing almost twice as often. In Jeremiah's time the Northern Kingdom of Israel had already been taken captive, so the term "Israel" is usually used in the broader sense of God's people still living in Canaan, the exceptions being references to the past before Israel's captivity (e.g., 3:8).

followed after God and reveled in His love and fellowship now had gone far from Him (2:5). And not only were the laity guilty of breaking the love ties, but also the leaders: priests, teachers of the law, rulers, and prophets (2:8).

b. *A Degenerate Vine* (God's "Why?" to evil choices, 2:9-25). The import of these verses of many interrogations (ten in the American Standard Version) may be summarized by one question, which actually implies exclamation, "Why have my people left the good and gone after the bad!" What corrupted mentality is here! According to the first paragraph (2:9-13) of this section, Israel had given up her glory for *that which did not profit* (2:11). How astonishing and horrifying that she should forsake a continuous fountain of living waters for broken cisterns that could hold no water (2:13).

In the second paragraph (2:14-19) another corrupt choice of Israel is scored. God sees His people as servants, slaves, and prey of other nations (2:14-16). But they were not that originally. They were once a people who were enjoying freedom and liberty. But they had chosen servitude to man, getting politically involved with either Egypt to the south,[5] or Assyria to the north (2:18). Israel had asked for trouble ("Hast thou not procured this unto thyself?" 2:17). God's big question is "Why does a people choose the bad?"

Still another example is given in the third paragraph (2:20-25). God, on His part, had planted Israel a noble vine, "a choice vine of completely reliable stock" (2:21, Berkeley Version). How then did they turn into degenerate branches ("bastard shoots," Berkeley) of an alien

---

[5]Memphis and Tahpanhes (2:16) were famous towns in northern and southern Egypt, respectively.

vine, bearing poisonous berries (2:21)? Concerning their iniquity, (1) their sins were deeper than surface dirt, unwashable by lye or soap (2:22); (2) they could not deny their sin (2:23); and (3) their lust for pleasure and flirting with strangers had blinded their eyes to the judgments for sin—pictured here in the bareness of foot and dryness of throat of a wild desert donkey (2:25, Berkeley).

c. A Caught Thief (God's judgment for persistent sin, 2:26-37). Now God spoke of the future. Tomorrow always catches up with the sinner. When Israel would be found as a thief in her shame (2:26), and when the time of trouble would come, then she would cry to God, "Arise, and save us" (2:27). God's answer was to be a cutting indictment for her former adulterous ways: "Where are thy gods that thou hast made thee? Let them arise, if they can save thee" (2:28).

In that future day of recompense for sins, the sins were to be identified. Among them would be (1) refusal to receive correction (2:30), (2) forgetting God "days without number" (2:32), and (3) gadding about to court the favor of men and nations (2:36).

The future judgments were inevitable as Judah persisted in the sins about which she had been warned. That there was a possibility of returning to Jehovah before the judgment which was to come, is the main thrust of the next of Jehovah's oracles delivered by Jeremiah.

2. *A Call to Return unto God* (3:1—4:4)[6]

Jeremiah had just exposed the people of God; they had gone far from their God and had kept their backs turned to Him. This was one of Jeremiah's "pluck up" warnings, addressed to the people's conscience. Now he had the

[6]Paragraphs at 3:1,6,11,19,22*b*; 4:1.

brighter though no less difficult task of delivering a "build and plant" message, addressed to the people's will. Its note of hope lies in God's invitation to return. The key phrase connecting both messages is in 3:12: "Return, thou backsliding Israel." The word *return* appears ten times in this oracle.

The first verse introduces the theme. God's law (Deut. 24:1-4) forbade a wife, divorced by her first husband and married to another, to return to her first love. Though Israel was in the same position as such a woman, for she had "played the harlot with many lovers," yet she was offered one last opportunity to return to her "husband." This is the sun of God's grace outshining the searchlight of God's law.

a. Return unto Me Wholeheartedly, Not Feignedly (3:2-10). Judah had *appeared to* return to God in the past, but it had not been with a whole heart; rather, the act had been feigned (3:10). God through Jeremiah cited an example. Judah had polluted the land with her wickedness, and God had sent judgment by withholding the crop-producing rains (3:2-3). Bowed by judgment, Judah had repented, outwardly at least: "Have you not just now cried to Me, 'My Father, Thou art a friend from my youth'?" (3:4, Berkeley Version). But these were mere words disguising evil deeds: "See, you have spoken [thus], but you have done all the evil you could do" (3:5, Berkeley).

It is very likely that Jeremiah was referring to Josiah's early reforms when he marked the sham of Judah's intentions (cf. 3:6a). On the surface the people had made good resolutions to fear God and to walk in His ways, but deep down in the heart they wanted to live in their old paths of sin. So the help of national decree or corporate action did

26

not avail. Nor had the example of the judgment of the northern tribes of Israel profited them.[7] Israel had sinned (3:6), had refused to return to God (3:7), and had been put away in bondage (3:8), and faithless Judah had seen it all happen to her sister, "but she also went and played the harlot" (3:8). If she ever spoke of returning, it was only pretention, surely not of the heart (3:10).

b. Return unto Me for Future Restoration (3:11-18). Now Jeremiah projects on the screen God's future plans of blessing for His chosen people. However, the blessing was conditioned on the returning. "You return in heart, 'and I will bring you to Zion,' corporately," is the intent of 3:14. This promise was given to both houses, Israel and Judah (cf. 3:18). But when Jeremiah spoke these words, Israel had already been taken captive into the northern land of Assyria. Was there hope for her? Yes: "Go, and proclaim these words toward the north, and say, Return, thou backsliding Israel," by acknowledging iniquity and disobedience (3:12-13). A return of heart was called for to bring blessings that would culminate in the inheritance of the next life. The near future, in the foreknowledge of God, was to be very dark for Judah and Israel. True, there would be a time of restoration and rebuilding the temple, with revivals of heart. But on the whole, the generations of God's people would be generations of stony hearts (cf. Malachi), eventually rejecting the Messiah, Christ. Beyond this, however, in the far, far future, there was a bright picture. God through Jeremiah portrays a touching scene of returners-in-heart when Judah and Israel, led by God (3:14), would walk together out of foreign lands

[7]In this paragraph (6-10) "Israel" refers to the Northern Kingdom, while "Judah" refers to the Southern Kingdom.

back to the land of inheritance (3:18). The things of the old covenant would give way to glories of the new (3:16), proceeding from the throne of Jehovah in Jerusalem, to which even Gentiles would gather and around which there would be found no evil (3:17).

Six centuries after Jeremiah delivered this promise of God to Judah and Israel, Paul was inspired to expand the truth in Romans 11, and practically two millennia later the prophecy of the regathering to Palestine has begun its fulfillment.

c. Return unto Me in Contrition (3:10-25). True returning had earlier been identified negatively as being unfeigned (3:5,10). Now its positive character of heart contrition is shown. A moving dramatic dialogue runs through the verses thus:

1) God asks, in effect, "How shall I give you this wonderful heritage, seeing that you have rejected Me?" (3:19a).[8]

2) God answers His own question, "I can do it if you will call Me 'my Father,' and not turn away from Me" (3:19b).

3) God turns to His people and says, "You have dealt faithlessly with Me. Return, and I will heal your backslidings" (3:20-22a).

4) The people respond by confessing their sin, "Behold, we come to You. You are our God. We vainly sought help elsewhere; salvation only comes from You. We have sinned against You, we have not obeyed Your voice" (3:22b-25).

d. Return unto Me for Present Deliverance (4:1-4). If Israel had acknowledged her sin as the dialogue above dramatized, then the command of 3:13 would have been

---

[8]American Standard and Berkeley Versions represent 19a as an exclamation.

a. The Untaught Laity and the Taught Leaders (5:1-6).
Jeremiah first sought out the common masses. Surely here
he should have found a righteous people, unspoiled by the
ride and self-sufficiency of power, wealth, and wisdom.
ut he found that "they have refused to receive correction:
y have made their faces harder than a rock" (5:3).
ncluding that it was because they had not been in-
ted in the law of God, Jeremiah decided, "I will get
nto the great men," the leaders and teachers who had
aught the way and law of God (5:5). "But these"
l had severed their relationship with God (5:5)
d increased in their backslidings (5:6).

e *Covenant Signers and Covenant Preachers* (5:7-
at about those who had once sincerely entered
enant with God, to swear by it to keep it? From
me, renewals of the original Sinaitic covenant
individually or in groups. If the words of this
e spoken after the discovery of the Book of
temple, then the covenant consecration of
under Josiah could be Jeremiah's reference.
case, people who had once entered into a
e now found swearing "by them that are

preachers, the prophets, were found to
Representing both houses, Israel and
ts had denied God ("It is not he") and
ither shall evil come upon us," 5:12).
s of wind, deniers of the true Word,
ies of whatever godly remnant dwelt
Contrast them with the true prophet,

of 5:7b in the American Standard Ver-
e them swear."

32

---

fulfilled, and God could have spared the people the impending woe about to break over them. They would not
have been removed (4:1), nor would God's wrath have
gone forth like fire (4:4). But the condition was as God
said, "If thou wilt return unto me!"

3. *Woes of the Judgment from the North* (4:5-31)[9]
Jeremiah's first sermon was one of denunciation of
backsliding Israel. The second gave an invitation, "Return
unto me." The third is one of visitation, describing the
forthcoming visitation of God's wrath upon His people
for their sin. The sermon is introduced by nine ominous
commands compacted into two verses, anticipating the
conqueror from the North. The exclamatory expressions
are: declare, publish, say, blow, cry aloud, assemble, set
up, flee, and stay not.

a. The Woes Are Seen in the Invaders' Assignments
(4:5-18). Three emblems symbolized the assignments of
the coming Babylonian invaders: *lion, hot wind,* and
watchers. The lion (4:7-9) was to come from his thicket to
tear apart the people as a nation. He was a "destroyer of
nations" (4:7) coming to lay waste cities (4:7), to disrupt
all leadership—kings, princes, prophets (4:9), and to take
away all national peace (4:10).

The hot wind (4:11-13) was to come from the bare
heights to lay bare, ruin, and antagonize the people's life
and livelihood. The hot wind is the fearful sirocco east
wind of the spring or fall season, associated with an air
mass which descends on Palestine from the upper atmosphere and remains for three to seven days. The unwelcome winds bring abnormally hot, dry, and dust-laden
air. The effects on the people are severe, causing irritability

---

[9]Paragraphs at 5, 11, 14, 19, 27.

29

of temper and physical pain and discomfort for many. The early spring crops are destroyed, and possessions are damaged by the dryness and dust.[10] By the emblem of the sirocco wind the invasion by the Chaldeans was prophesied to be destructive to the life and livelihood of the people (a wind "not to winnow, nor to cleanse," 4:11, "we are ruined," 4:13). The hordes of invaders were to come down swiftly and in clouds of dust ("his chariots shall be as the whirlwind: his horses are swifter than eagles," 4:13).

Watchers ("besiegers," Berkeley) were to come from a far country, staking out the holy city and watching movements within its walls, waiting for the strategic moment to strike. The watchers symbolize the eyes of the divine Judge who sees the thoughts, desires, and motives of the heart, and determines the moment of execution of judgment. Evil thoughts and a people with wicked and rebellious hearts (4:17-18) were lodging in Jerusalem (4:14), and if she were to be saved from the eyes of the watchers, Jeremiah warned, she had to wash her heart from wickedness (4:14).

b. *The Woes Are Seen in Jeremiah's Anguish* (4:19-26). Deep pangs of pain pierce Jeremiah's heart as he ponders the impending woes. "My anguish, my anguish! I am pained at my very heart; my heart is disquieted in me; I cannot hold my peace" (4:19). Jeremiah's anguish was caused by (1) the inevitable fact of total and sudden destruction (4:20; see also the four visions "I beheld" in

[10]Compare Isaiah 27:8; 40:6-8; Ezekiel 17:10; Hosea 13:5; Luke 12:55; and James 1:11 for other references to this strange and destructive wind. Also see Denis Baly, *The Geography of the Bible* (New York: Harper and Brothers, 1957), pp. 67-70, for further description of the sirocco wind.

verses 23-26) and (2) the inexcusable folly of his "They are wise to do evil, but to do good they knowledge" (4:22).

c. *The Woes Are Seen in the Unalterable* God (4:27-31). The divine decree was firs whole land shall be a desolation" (4-27a) parenthetical statement that followed ("y a full end") was intended to show that tion and captivity were not to mark history of the city (Jerusalem) or Having pronounced the content then stated the unalterable cha have purposed it . . . neither (4:28). Two vain attempts o to change His mind are th ternal prettiness (4:30), cere heart; and (2) th (4:31) which God wi after the day of optio

The sermon had safety!" It closed for my soul fain

4. *Exposu* Jerusalem from witho working f streets o lived j prop

fulfilled, and God could have spared the people the impending woe about to break over them. They would not have been removed (4:1), nor would God's wrath have gone forth like fire (4:4). But the condition was as God said, "If thou wilt return unto me!"

3. *Woes of the Judgment from the North* (4:5-31)[9] Jeremiah's first sermon was one of denunciation of backsliding Israel. The second gave an invitation, "Return unto me." The third is one of visitation, describing the forthcoming visitation of God's wrath upon His people for their sin. The sermon is introduced by nine ominous commands compacted into two verses, anticipating the conqueror from the North. The exclamatory expressions are: declare, publish, say, blow, cry aloud, assemble, set up, flee, and stay not.

a. *The Woes Are Seen in the Invaders' Assignments* (4:5-18). Three emblems symbolized the assignments of the coming Babylonian invaders: *lion, hot wind,* and *watchers.* The lion (4:7-9) was to come from his thicket to tear apart the people as a nation. He was a "destroyer of nations" (4:7) coming to lay waste cities (4:7), to disrupt all leadership—kings, princes, prophets (4:9), and to take away all national peace (4:10).

The hot wind (4:11-13) was to come from the bare heights to lay bare, ruin, and antagonize the people's life and livelihood. The hot wind is the fearful sirocco east wind of the spring or fall season, associated with an air mass which descends on Palestine from the upper atmosphere and remains for three to seven days. The unwelcome winds bring abnormally hot, dry, and dust-laden air. The effects on the people are severe, causing irritability

---

[9]Paragraphs at 5, 11, 14, 19, 27.

of temper and physical pain and discomfort for many. The early spring crops are destroyed, and possessions are damaged by the dryness and dust.[10] By the emblem of the sirocco wind the invasion by the Chaldeans was prophesied to be destructive to the life and livelihood of the people (a wind "not to winnow, nor to cleanse," 4:11, "we are ruined," 4:13). The hordes of invaders were to come down swiftly and in clouds of dust ("his chariots shall be as the whirlwind: his horses are swifter than eagles," 4:13).

Watchers ("besiegers," Berkeley) were to come from a far country, staking out the holy city and watching movements within its walls, waiting for the strategic moment to strike. The watchers symbolize the eyes of the divine Judge who sees the thoughts, desires, and motives of the heart, and determines the moment of execution of judgment. Evil thoughts and a people with wicked and rebellious hearts (4:17-18) were lodging in Jerusalem (4:14), and if she were to be saved from the eyes of the watchers, Jeremiah warned, she had to wash her heart from wickedness (4:14).

b. The Woes Are Seen in Jeremiah's Anguish (4:19-26). Deep pangs of pain pierce Jeremiah's heart as he ponders the impending woes. "My anguish, my anguish! I am pained at my very heart; my heart is disquieted in me; I cannot hold my peace" (4:19). Jeremiah's anguish was caused by (1) the inevitable fact of total and sudden destruction (4:20; see also the four visions "I beheld" in

---

[10]Compare Isaiah 27:8; 40:6-8; Ezekiel 17:10; Hosea 13:5; Luke 12:55; and James 1:11 for other references to this strange and destructive wind. Also see Denis Baly, *The Geography of the Bible* (New York: Harper and Brothers, 1957), pp. 67-70, for further description of the sirocco wind.

verses 23-26) and (2) the inexcusable folly of his people: "They are wise to do evil, but to do good they have no knowledge" (4:22).

c. The Woes Are Seen in the Unalterable Purposes of God (4:27-31). The divine decree was first stated: "The whole land shall be a desolation" (4-27*a*). The qualifying parenthetical statement that followed ("yet will I not make a full end") was intended to show that the coming destruction and captivity were not to mark the end of the long history of the city (Jerusalem) or of the people (Judah). Having pronounced the content of the decree, Jeremiah then stated the unalterable character of the decree: "I have purposed it . . . neither will I turn back from it" (4:28). Two vain attempts of the people to persuade God to change His mind are then cited: (1) the lure of external prettiness (4:30), e.g., pretty words but not a sincere heart; and (2) the lure of a pitiable cry for help (4:31) which God will hear but ignore, for it will come after the day of options has passed.

The sermon had opened with the warning, "Flee for safety!" It closed with the cry of death: "Woe is me now! for my soul fainteth before the murderers."

4. *Exposure of the Enemies from Within* (5:1-31)[11]

Jerusalem was to fall at the hands of the political enemy from without because of the spiritual enemies of God working from within.[12] God had Jeremiah scouring the streets of the city to see if he could find one man who lived justly and sought truth (5:1). The report of the prophet's search is the theme of this sermon.

[11]Paragraphs at 1,5,7,10,14,20,30.

[12]The section 4:5—6:30 alternates in its description of these enemies: without, 4:5-31; within, 5:1-14; without, 5:15-19; within, 5:20-31; without, 6:1-8; within, 6:9-21; without, 6:22-30.

31

a. The Untaught Laity and the Taught Leaders (5:1-6).
Jeremiah first sought out the common masses. Surely here
he should have found a righteous people, unspoiled by the
pride and self-sufficiency of power, wealth, and wisdom.
But he found that "they have refused to receive correction:
they have made their faces harder than a rock" (5:3).
Concluding that it was because they had not been instructed in the law of God, Jeremiah decided, "I will get
me unto the great men," the leaders and teachers who had
been taught the way and law of God (5:5). "But these"
as well had severed their relationship with God (5:5)
and had increased in their backslidings (5:6).

b. The Covenant Signers and Covenant Preachers (5:7-
19.) What about those who had once sincerely entered
into a covenant with God, to swear by it to keep it? From
time to time, renewals of the original Sinaitic covenant
were made individually or in groups. If the words of this
chapter were spoken after the discovery of the Book of
Law in the temple, then the covenant consecration of
II Kings 23:3 under Josiah could be Jeremiah's reference.
Whatever the case, people who had once entered into a
covenant[13] were now found swearing "by them that are
no gods" (5:7a).

The covenant preachers, the prophets, were found to
be just as guilty. Representing both houses, Israel and
Judah, the prophets had denied God ("It is not he") and
the judgment ("Neither shall evil come upon us," 5:12).
They were prophets of wind, deniers of the true Word,
and influential enemies of whatever godly remnant dwelt
within Judah (5:13). Contrast them with the true prophet,

---

[13]The alternate reading of 5:7b in the American Standard Version is "when I had made them swear."

32

Jeremiah, who spoke God's words of fire (5:14), warning of the mighty, ancient nation, Chaldea, coming to devour the fields and the cities (5:15-18) and to take the people captive to serve strangers in a foreign land, even as they were serving foreign gods in their own land (5:19).

c. Breakers of God's Boundaries and Overpassers in Wickedness (5:20-31). The sea does not—yea, cannot—break the general boundaries of shoreline[14] set by God in perpetual decree (5:22). But God's people had revolted and "gone over" the boundaries placed around them by God's Word (5:23-25). Likewise, the "big-time operators" —that host of the great, rich, deceitful, and self-indulgent —had overpassed in deeds of wickedness, pouncing upon even the innocent fatherless (5:26-31).

The leaven of unrighteousness had so utterly pervaded the entire kingdom of God's people that in reporting his findings, Jeremiah made this pungent summation:

> Astonishing and horrible is the state of our nation:
> The PROPHETS prophesy falsely;
> The PRIESTS rule presumptuously,[15]
> And the PEOPLE *love to have it so!*

5. *A City to Be Visited* (6:1-30)[16]

"Cast up a mound against Jerusalem: this is the city to be visited" (6:6). Again and again, Jeremiah had to declare the words of impending doom. This message was no exception. The source of the decree was always Jehovah: "Thus saith Jehovah of hosts" (6:9). The precise agent

---

[14]This illustration is stated by the prophet from the standpoint of appearance to the observer, in what may be called "phenomenal language." See Bernard Ramm, *Protestant Biblical Interpretation* (Boston: W. A. Wilde Company, 1956), pp. 191-92.

[15]"According to their own hands," Berkeley Version.

[16]Paragraphs at 1,9,16,22,27.

of execution of the decree was Chaldea,[17] the evil nation from the North (6:1,22). The object of the decree was invariably Judah and Jerusalem. The intimately involved messenger of the decree was God's chosen prophet, Jeremiah. Early in this discourse the searchlight of attention was aimed at the city of Jerusalem and its inhabitants. "This is the city," God said, "that must be visited with great destruction."

a. A Forewarned City (6:1-8). Jerusalem was not without forewarning. "Flee for safety" are the first three words of the discourse. Life could have been spared thereby though bondage to the foe was inevitable. Zealous and intent were the coming invaders, whom even the shades of evening would not daunt (6:3-5). Verse 8 is the bright note of this paragraph. The "lest" holds out hope of reversing the divine decree of destruction (6:6): "Be thou instructed, O Jerusalem, LEST my soul be alienated from thee; LEST I make thee a desolation, a land not inhabited" (6:8).

b. An Abominable City (6:9-21). The prophet first questioned why he should be speaking to people who *would not* hear, to whom the word of God had absolutely no attraction (6:10). Then he acknowledged why he must speak: he had been made to be full of God's wrath; he could not hold back the words any longer; they had to be poured out upon the people, even as the judgment itself would be poured out (6:11). The wrath was for sins of covetousness (6:13), false leadership (6:13-14), abomination (6:15), stubbornness and rejection of the law (6:16-19), and false sacrifices (6:20). Then, like a pure

---

[17]The exact identification of the enemy from the North is not made in the early chapters of this prophecy. The Babylonians are first mentioned in 20:4, and the Chaldeans in 21:4.

spring of water rising into a muddy pool, God's appeal of 6:16 and 17 stands in the midst of the list of sins. The appeal is for the people to ask for the "old paths"—the good ways walked in by righteous men of old—and to walk therein to find soul rest. It was a tender appeal from a long-suffering God, but the people's response was a tragic shout of defiance: "We will not!"

c. A Mourning City (6:22-26). In a pattern of alternation, Jeremiah's words revert again to the "great nation" from the North. The invaders were cruel and merciless (6:23), formidable and fearful (6:23-25). "For this," cried the prophet, "gird thee with sackcloth, and wallow thyself in ashes: make thee mourning, as for an only son, most bitter lamentation" (6:26). The first paragraph of this discourse ended with an invitation of hope. This paragraph denotes anticipation that the invitation was to be rejected; hence its last verse is one of mourning for the irreversible judgment.

d. A Tried City (6:27-30). The discourse ends with the graphic, figurative truth of God's attempts to purge His people of their sinful ways. Three pictures are given, each related to metals. In the first, God told Jeremiah one of his tasks: "I have made you an assayer and examiner among my peoples, so that you may test and analyze their actions" (6:27, Berkeley Version). In the second, the people were likened to brass and iron, representing impudence and obstinacy, respectively (6:28).[18] In the third and most important picture, the people were likened to contaminated silver which has been subjected to the refining process to carry away the impurities, but which at the end of the unsuccessful process is still impure. The

---

[18]Berkeley Version, footnote o, in location.

Berkeley Version gives this pertinent background: "In refining, the goldsmith mixes lead with the alloy containing the gold or silver, fused in a furnace on a vessel of earth or bone ash; a current of air is turned upon the molten mass [not upon the fire]; the lead then oxidizes and, acting as a flux, carries away the alloy, leaving the pure gold or silver."[19]

"*Refuse* silver they are called, because the Lord has *refused* them" (6:30, Berkeley).[20]

6. *False Trusts That Cannot Profit* (7:1—8:3)[21] (First Charge of Temple Discourse)

Most, if not all, of chapters 7 to 20 relate to the days of the reign of Jehoiakim.[22] This cruel and selfish despot[23] was a vassal of Egypt until Egyptian power in Syria and Palestine was crushed at the Battle of Carchemish (605 B.C.), and Jehoiakim became subject to Babylon. Jeremiah's faith, courage, patience, and vision were utterly tried during these years because of the people and their king. The messages recorded in these chapters reveal much of those trials.

During Jehoiakim's reign the prophet delivered a message (or series of messages) centered on temple worship, which has been called "The Temple Discourse" (7:1—10:25). Chapter 26, if taken to refer to the same discourse because of its similarities, records the reactions and sequels which the discourse brought about, when Jeremiah was put on trial for his life.

[19]*Ibid.*, footnote p.
[20]The italicized words are of identical roots in the Hebrew text.
[21]Paragraphs at 1,12,16,21,29; 8:1.
[22]Chapters 11 and 12 may be dated in Josiah's reign, chapter 13 in Jehoiachin's reign. See Howard T. Kuist, "The Book of Jeremiah," *Interpretation,* July, 1950, pp. 329-30.
[23]Refer to II Kings 23:31—24:7; II Chronicles 36:1-8 for historical references to the reign of Jehoiakim.

36

Jeremiah's frequent references to the temple building (e.g., "temple of Jehovah," 7:4; "this house which is called by my name," 7:10), made as he stood "in the gate of Jehovah's house" proclaiming the word, give reason for the title of the discourse. The charges which the prophet made therein against the people show how ineffective or temporary were the recent reforms of King Josiah. The first charge (7:1—8:3) was against false trusts that "cannot profit" (7:8). In chapter 7, three such false trusts are exposed (7:1-28), and the awful judgments which they were to bring are described (7:29—8:3).

a. Trusting in Religion (7:1-15). Trusting in religion cannot profit. The temple building itself had become the people's object of worship, replacing the *Person* of the building. The people, taught by the false prophets, regarded the temple as an automatic visible seal of invincibility, for could a foreign nation destroy the house belonging to *God?* Hence, born to this religion of externals was the first religious chant:

> "The temple of Jehovah,
> The temple of Jehovah,
> The temple of Jehovah" (7:4).

But this chant originated with false prophets who lied, hence the "lying words that cannot profit" (7:8).

The second empty religious chant was, "We are delivered" (7:10), words which were also described as "lying words" (7:8). In everyday life the people freely sinned—they stole, murdered, committed adultery, swore falsely, and worshiped other gods (7:9)—and then, at the "religious" hour of the day and week, they came to stand before God in the house which was called by His name, and in a religious ritual of lip-worship they chanted in a "religious" monotone, "We are delivered," expecting thereby to receive automatic indulgence for their abominations (7:10-11). In reality, they had turned God's house of worship into a hangout of criminals, the very situation which was to confront Jesus centuries later (cf. Matt. 21:13; Mark 11:17; Luke 19:46).

b. Trusting in Heathen Gods (7:16-20) This is another false trust that could not profit. The scene of the sin of false trust changed from the temple to the streets (7:17), more specifically to each house of the Israelite families. If God had ever been worshiped in the home before, He had now been replaced by heroes and idols. In enthusiastic family spirit, everyone showed his devotion to the "Queen of heaven" (an ancient Semitic deity, the Babylonian Ishtar[24]): the children gathered wood, the fathers kindled the fire, and the women kneaded dough to make cakes for the Queen (7:18). Added to this worship were the drink offerings poured out to other gods (7:18). So abominable was the heart of the people at this stage that it was as though the judgment had already come, and therefore intercession for them was interdicted (7:16).

c. Trusting in Self (7:21-28). In trusting in burnt offerings and sacrifices, the people were guilty of ritual by rote, devoid of heart worship. Down through generations of their forefathers, God had consistently appealed to heart-trust, which was the way of salvation for all ages, whether before (e.g., the exodus, 7:22), during (in Canaan), or after the times of Old Testament offerings. In His long-suffering and mercy, God daily took the initiative and, "rising up early," sent His prophets to His people with

[24]Cf. 44:17-19,25.

this message, "Hearken unto me" (7:23-25). Jeremiah was one whom He so sent (7:27-28). The people's response was almost to a man: "We will not hearken unto You; we will go our way, in our own counsels" (7:24). And with unbent ears, stiff necks, and reversed steps (7:24,26) they rejected God to trust in themselves.

d. The Judgments (7:29—8:3). The penalty for false trust (7:30-31) was terrible judgment, which mourning and lamentation could only acknowledge, surely not soothe (7:29). Jeremiah shows that the judgments would reflect the sin of idolatry:

1) As Topheth was the place of idolatrous child sacrifice, so it would become the valley of slaughter in the day of judgment, lacking burial space for the hosts of corpses (7:31-33).

2) As the people worshiped and adored the celestial bodies, the day of judgment would see the people's bones disinterred and spread out on the earth, under the skies of their gods, but in vain (8:1-2).

For those spared death, the judgments would spoil the very experience of living: mirth and gladness would vanish away (7:34), and life itself would be despaired of (8:3). *The fruit of false trusts is bitter.*

7. *Rejection of God's Word* (8:4-17)[25] (Second Charge of Temple Discourse)

The temple and the law were inseparable in Israel's worship. It was therefore inevitable that Jeremiah would deliver a charge about the law, God's written Word to His people, in the temple messages.

a. The People Reject the Word (8:4-7). When Jeremiah lamented, "My people know not the law of Jehovah"

---
[25]Paragraphs at 4,8,13.

(8:7), he used the word *know* in the sense of "live by" or "obey." This is borne out by the context: (1) the migratory birds (stork, turtledove, swallow, crane) know their "appointed times," that is, they live by and obey the instincts of migratory times of departures and arrivals; (2) the people were described as having disobedient hearts, refusing to return (8:5), when they should have been rising up again out of their fallen condition (8:4).

b. *God's Ministers Do Not Teach the Word* (8:8-12). Dark is the day when people reject God's Word. Darker it is when the ministers of the Word betray their holy commission. The people could not boast wisdom for having the law of God when they were being taught a false interpretation of it. Those guilty of transmitting this false interpretation were the scribes, who wrote falsely (8:8), and the prophets and priests, who spoke falsely (e.g., preaching, "Peace, peace, when there is no peace," 8:10-11).

c. *Doom Is Inevitable* (8:13-17). God's pronouncements of judgment were brief: "I will utterly consume" (8:13), and "I will send serpents" (8:17). Between those words are the futile moans of a people resigned to destruction, who would flee to the best man-made shelter, a fortress, to avoid a measure of ignominy, and to perish with "pride": "Why do we sit still? . . . let us enter into the fortified cities, and let us *perish* there" (8:14, italicized word found in the margin, A.S.V.).

8. *The Prophet's Lament: We Are Not Saved!* (8:18—9:26)[26] (Third Charge of Temple Discourse)

At this point in his temple message Jeremiah breaks out into heartrending lamentation and crying for his

---

[26]Paragraphs at 8:18; 9:1,7,10,12,17,23,25.

40

doomed people, uttering such pitiful words as "The harvest is past, the summer is ended, and we are not saved." Throughout this charge the themes of lamentation and the answers of Jehovah alternate, especially with regard to judgment, in the following pattern: lamentation (8:18—9:6), reason for judgment (9:7-9); lamentation (9:10-11), reason for judgment (9:12-16); lamentation (9:17-22), final words of Jehovah (saving glory, 9:23-24, and ultimate judgment, 9:25-26).

a. First Lamentation (8:18—9:6). Two things crushed the heart of the prophet. First was the fact that his people's lost state was unnecessary because grace from heaven was at their disposal: Jehovah their King was in Zion, and there was more than ample spiritual balm and the Physician to apply it for Israel's healing (8:19, 22). Second was the utter degradation of the heart of his people, so abominable that the prophet longed to be separated from them, shepherd though he was (9:2). (See vv. 2-6 for the description of their evil hearts.)

God's answer to Jeremiah's lamentation reveals the righteous aspect of the divine judgment (9:7-9). For deceit there must be judgment. No alternative exists. "How else should I do?" is God's emphatic response (9:7).

b. Second Lamentation (9:10-11). Now the prophet lamented the desolation of the land and everything in it: the mountains and pastures, the cattle, birds, and beasts, the holy city Jerusalem, and all the cities round about.

God's answer to the question (implied in the lament of 9:10-11 and now stated explicitly) *"Why* is the land perished and burned up?" is very comprehensive. The judgment was for forsaking His law, disobedience, stubbornness, and idolatry, or Baalim worship (9:13-14).

41

c. Third Lamentation (9:17-22). The third and last lamentation is the death dirge. An urgent call is sent out for the skillfull professional women wailers (9:17-18), for "death is come up into our windows" (9:21). "How are we ruined!" is the wailing chant of the living bereaved (9:19).

Jehovah's answer to this lamentation was also a climactic summary to the entire charge, identifying two universal truths. The first of these is that salvation is for all who *know* God (9:23-24). He whose greatest passion is merely wisdom, or might, or riches, is lost. But he whose greatest passion (and therefore glory) is to know God intimately and experientially, is saved.

The second universal truth is that judgment is for all who are unbelievers *in heart* (9:25-26). Not only Judah but also Egypt, Edom, Ammon, and Moab would be judged (9:26). In fact, all nations with unbelieving hearts (which is the intent of the phrase "uncircumcised in heart") must be so punished.

The utter despair of the prophet is understandable in view of the fact that though he must and would preach repentance to his people, he knew that they had reached the point of no return as far as their salvation was concerned. Earlier in his preaching he had exhorted his people to return to God. Those were days of the season of hope. Jeremiah would continue to plead for repentance,[27] but with prophetic foresight he views the spiritual harvest period as being past, the time of the gathering of summer fruits as being ended, neither season having

---

[27]Toward the end of his ministry, just before the fall of Jerusalem, Jeremiah emphasized the *sureness of* the coming judgment, but pleaded with the people to obey the Word of God in order to ameliorate the judgment.

yielded spiritual fruit. Spiritual famine was the future of Judah. "We are not saved!" is the sad lament.

9. *None Like Jehovah* (10:1-25)[28] (Final Charge of Temple Discourse)

At this point the temple discourse closes with a majestic note, exalting Jehovah as God of all. He is called the "King of the nations" (10:7), the "true God . . . the living God . . . everlasting King" (10:10), "Jehovah of hosts" (10:16); and twice Jeremiah says of Him, "There is none like unto thee" (10:6-7). The broad scope of God's relationships is also emphasized here. He is shown in His relationships to nations (10:1-11), to nature (10:12-13), and to mankind (10:14-25).

a. There Is No Other God (10:1-5). The heathen nations, in their fear of potentially destructive elements of nature (e.g., the bolt of lightning), and in their dependency on favoring elements (e.g., rain for the crops), manufactured hosts of gods accordingly, fashioning them out of the trees of the forest (10:3), and decking them with silver and gold (10:4). But such gods were speechless, immobile, and impotent (10:5), and Jehovah warned that the vanity of the nations making the gods must not be embraced by Israel (10:2).

b. There Is No Greater Power on Earth (10:6-11). Jeremiah continued his proclamation: God is King over all nations; He is great in might (10:6-7). Among all the wise men of the nations, and in all their royal estate, there is none like Jehovah (10:7). The greatest earthly nation was Lilliputian when measured by the lifeless and impotent idols which its people worshiped as their superiors. To such nations Jeremiah delivered this divine message of

---

[28]Paragraphs at 1,6,12,17,19,23.

highest diplomatic importance (hence the fact that 10:11 is recorded in Aramaic, the language of international diplomacy in Jeremiah's day): "The gods that have not made the heavens and the earth . . . shall perish from the earth, and from under the heavens" (10:11). But Jehovah is the true God, the living One, the everlasting King.

c. There Is No Other Cause Behind the Universe (10:12-16). God made the earth by His power, the world by His wisdom, and the heavens by His understanding (10:12). Graven images, by the very fact of their being made by brutish men without knowledge, could not compete with Him (10:14-15).

d. There is No Like Sovereign Judge (10:17-25). No voice could thwart God's sovereign execution of judgment. Those spared destruction would have to obey divine orders (10:17). The wails of unrepentant hearts would not move Him to reverse His judgment (10:19-22). Justifiable petitions could be made to Him (10:24-25), but in the last analysis, "it is not in man . . . to direct his steps" (10:23). This is the absolute prerogative of the sovereign Lord.

Thus Jeremiah's last public discourse of this series ended on a high note. As the prophet saw the divine judgments in the light of the exalted Person as Judge, he was able to rise to this height of exalting spirit from the depths of despair of his previous messages.

* * *

The nine public messages of the foregoing series had brought to the people the words of denunciation (messages 1, 4, 6, 7), invitation (2), visitation (3,5), lamentation (8), and exaltation (9). Jeremiah's lips had not been closed yet, however. God continued to give him words to speak, especially as they were born in the prophet's personal experiences.

B. Personal Experiences (11:1—20:18)

The preceding chapters (2-10) record the messages delivered by the prophet on the street and in the temple, without any particular reference to his own personal experiences. Now in chapters 11 through 20 his personal trials and problems are brought to light as they arose out of his faithfulness to the prophetic message. Most of these events transpired during Jehoiakim's reign, some ten to twenty years before Jerusalem was to be destroyed. It will be observed in the course of these chapters that often one personal experience introduced many associated truths in Jeremiah's prophetic message.

1. *Covenant and Conspiracy*: *Jeremiah and the Men of Anathoth* (11:1—12:17)[29]

Jeremiah was preaching the covenant of Jehovah, but he had to contend with conspiracies designed to break that very covenant, whether directly or indirectly. Chapters 11 and 12 together tell this story. The first two paragraphs of chapter 11 introduce the theme of the covenant; the paragraphs between speak of the conspiracies involved, and the last two paragraphs of chapter 12 give the final outcome.

a. The Covenant Stated (11:1-8). Jeremiah was told by God that his basic message to Judah was to be simply this: "Hear ye the words of this covenant" (notice the repetition in these verses). The covenant itself involved four facts: (1) God gave the Word, (2) Israel was to obey

---

[29]Paragraphs at 11:1,6,9,14,18; 12:1,5,7,14.

the Word, (3) Israel would then be God's people, and (4) Jehovah would be Israel's God (11:4). The first paragraph (11:1-5) contains a warning (a curse for not hearing 11:3) followed by the original historical setting of the command (11:4-5). The second paragraph (11:6-8) contains the positive command ("Hear ye," 11:6) followed by a warning taken from the same historical setting (11:7-8).

b. The Covenant Broken (11:9-13). This was the first of three conspiracies. "A conspiracy is found among the men of Judah" (11:9), that of turning from God to iniquity and therefore breaking the covenant (11:10). It was a national conspiracy against God, the judgment for which is described in the next paragraph (11:14-17).

c. The Covenant Preacher Threatened (11:18-23). When people reject God, they will also reject His messengers. Thus Jeremiah, the preacher of the covenant, was the object of the second conspiracy, instigated by men of Jeremiah's hometown, Anathoth. Seeking the life of the prophet because he prophesied in the name of Jehovah (11:21), they said, "Let us destroy the tree . . . and let us cut him off from the land of the living, that his name may be no more remembered" (11:19). Jeremiah's reaction was that of a "gentle lamb that is led to the slaughter" (11:19), for he knew that God Himself would judge the men (11:20). God reassured Jeremiah's confidence in Him by revealing His pronouncement of judgment: the men would die by the sword, their children would die by famine, and they would leave no remnant (11:22-23).

d. The Covenant Preacher's Question (12:1-6). The third conspiracy is revealed in the course of the dialogue between God and Jeremiah after the prophet, whose eye had not overlooked the fact of the present temporal prosperity of wicked men among whom must have been his own townspeople of Anathoth, had asked God the age-old question, "Why do the wicked prosper?" (12:1-2). The record of Jeremiah's expostulation with God reveals a measure of his human impatience. The Berkeley Version translates verse 1 thus: "Righteous art thou, O Lord, when I complain to Thee; yet will I argue with Thee about justice." Jeremiah in effect asked God to compare him with the wicked: "Thou knowest me . . . pull them out like sheep for the slaughter" (12:3). It is in God's reply (12:5-6) that the third conspiracy is revealed, that of the prophet's own family. "For even thy brethren, and the house of thy father . . . have dealt treacherously with thee" (12:6). No greater hurt could have come to the heart of the prophet.

   e. The Covenant Applied (12:7-17). The covenant's application brought one of two possible results: cursing for breaking it (11:3), or blessing for obeying it (11:4-5). This section of chapter 12 describes these two results. Since the covenant had been broken, Jehovah (through His spokesman Jeremiah) spoke the word which the broken covenant demanded: judgment. Jehovah was compelled to forsake His house and heritage and give them to the hand of their enemies (12:7). The executors of this judgment on Israel, namely the evil foreign nations, were responsible for their own personal evil, and so would also be punished (12:14). But after those nations had been "plucked up," God in His compassion would bring them back to their land, where they would share the blessing of God with the faithful remnant of Israel, if they learned the ways of that remnant, to swear by the name, "As Jehovah liveth" (12:16). The casting away of Israel thus would become the reconciling of the world (see Rom. 11:15). God's covenant with Israel was destined by divine design to bless the whole world!

The world today needs more Jeremiahs who, in the midst of opposition, are true to the standards of the Bible, patient in the proclamation of the gospel, gentle in the hands of persecutors, committed to the protective care of the Chief Shepherd, and burdened for the souls of lost men and women. Satan and the world may conspire against a servant of God, but the conspiracy is really against God, and *God is invincible!*

2. *Pride of Judah*: *Jeremiah and the Linen Girdle* (13:1-27).[30]

The subject of the haughty "pride of Judah, and the great pride of Jerusalem" (13:9) now comes into special focus in Jeremiah's prophecy, introduced by things the prophet was ordered of God to do in connection with a linen girdle.

The chapter has three sections: (1) the pride exposed, under the symbols of the girdle and the bottles (1-14), (2) the surrender of pride exhorted (15-17), and (3) the pride punished (18-27). The first section emphasizes the prophecy of the *fact* of judgment that was to come, while the last section places emphasis on *description* of the judgment.

a. *The Pride Exposed* (13:1-14). In the girdle episode, God was primarily speaking to Jeremiah of Judah's pride, though the prophet undoubtedly would relate this clear and unequivocal symbolic experience to his people in

---

[30]Paragraphs at 1,8,12,15,18,20.

the course of his preaching. Jeremiah was commanded to do three things to a linen girdle:

1) Buy and wear it (13:1-2). It was not to be put in water, probably meaning that it was to be dirty when the next disposition of it was to be made.

2) Hide it (13:3-5). Jeremiah was to hide it in a cleft of a rock, by the Euphrates.[31]

3) Recover it (13:6-7). After many days Jeremiah, commanded to recover the girdle, found it "marred . . . [and] profitable for nothing."

God very clearly interpreted the symbols for Jeremiah (13:9-11). As the girdle cleaves close to the body of a man, so God wanted Judah and Israel to cleave to Him "for a people . . . a name . . . a praise . . . a glory; but *they would not*" (13:11), because of their pride (13:9). Their rejection of this intimate relationship was to bring on their being hidden away until they would become marred and unprofitable in worship and service. The coming captivity was the intended meaning of the symbol.

The symbol of the bottles (or jars) prophesied a further aspect of judgment of the people's pride: beyond becoming unprofitable, they faced violent destruction (13:14). The jars were filled with the wine of God's indignation (cf. 25: 15), bringing on a spiritual and mental drunkenness (13:

---

[31]If the Hebrew word *Perath* means Euphrates, then the two very long journeys to this distant valley must have impressed the prophet as to the importance of the lesson being taught. Also, the geographical location would then have been a symbol of the location of the captivity to come (Babylon in the Euphrates Valley). The other more probable translation of *Perath* is represented thus in the footnote of the Berkeley Version: "Here it probably refers to 'Parah,' a town about three miles northeast of Anathoth [Josh. 18:23], located in a wild and rocky valley watered by a copious spring, Wady Fara, which runs into the Wady Kelt flowing down past Jericho into the Jordan."

13) and bewilderment in the face of sudden judgment, such as is described in 25:16: "They shall drink and stagger and be frantic, because of the sword which I am sending among them."

b. *Surrender of Pride Exhorted* (13:15-17). The exhortation is brief and succinct: Be willing to listen, don't be proud, give glory to God (13:15). If the people would fail to respond thus, gross darkness and death were to be their doom, and sore weeping was Jeremiah's burden (13:16-17).

c. *Pride Punished* (13:18-27). Detailed description of the impending judgment is now given in the context of the sin of pride already exposed. National punishment, involving the heads of the state (king and queen-mother, 13:18) is described first. "Humble yourselves, sit down; for your headtires are come down, even the crown of your glory" (13:18). This was to be fulfilled in the shutting up of the Negev cities of the South and the carrying away of all Judah (13:19). *"Lift up your eyes"* is the pride-judging phrase introducing the description of the onrushing judgment from the North (13:20-27).

The concluding word of the chapter is a fitting wail over a nation that was found guilty of pride, unwilling to let the Sun of righteousness melt its obstinate heart: "Woe unto thee, O Jerusalem! Thou wilt not . . ." (13:27).

3. *The Drought: Jeremiah as the Interceding Priest* (14:1-22)[32]

This "drought chapter" shows the most intense intercessory character of Jeremiah. The land was in the throes of severe drought (1-6); he confessed the sin of his people and pleaded mercy for them (7-9); he heard God's pro-

---

[32]Paragraphs at 1,7,10,13,19.

nouncement of rejection of the people and false prophets (10-18); and he again pleaded mercy on the basis of confession (19-22).

The drought which Jeremiah lamented in this chapter may have been knowledge of a future event, such as the drought which later brought on the famine of the siege of Jerusalem (II Kings 25:3). The more natural interpretation, however, is that the drought had already plagued the people, while the famine referred to in verses 12, 13, 15, 16 and 18 was to be the future judgment.

a. Present Drought (14:1-6). The drought brought languish and mourning to all levels of life of Judah from the highest to the lowest (14:2): to the nobles, who could not locate the priceless commodity of water; to the common masses, represented by the plowman who could not till the hard cracked earth; to the domestic flock, represented by the tender, motherly hind, who was compelled to forsake her young for want of grass; and to the wild animal kingdom, represented by the wild ass, whose eyes failed to the point of exhaustion for want of herbage (14:3-6).

b. First Intercession (14:7-9). Jeremiah, identifying himself with the people in a priestly role, interceded for God's help on the bases of: (1) admission of sin (14:7), (2) an interested God (not a disinterested traveler, 14:8), (3) an able God (not an affrighted man, 14:9), and (4) the presence of God—for the Israelites were still called by His name (14:9).

c. Future Famine (14:10-18). God acknowledged the prophet's intercession, but reminded him that the people were individually responsible for persistently loving to wander from Him (14:10), and that the fasting and

51

sacrifices of the people (14:12) were not from the heart. Therefore, Jeremiah was told not to pray that God would give "good" to the people (14:11); the sentence of sword, famine, and pestilence had already been imposed for their sin (14:12).

d. Second Intercession (14:13-18). Jeremiah could not cease from praying for his people. He entreated God to spare Judah since the people had been deceived by prophets promising peace (14:13). God's reply was strong. Those prophets were false prophets, lying in His name, and for this they were to be consumed by the sword and famine (14:15). But this in no way absolved the people who received their false teaching. They were likewise to be consumed (14:16).

e. Third Intercession (14:19-22). Jeremiah's continued intercession then reached a high pitch of emotion as well as a strong level of claim. His appeals were directed to: (1) *a tender physician*—"Hath thy soul loathed Zion? Why. . . is no healing for us?" (14:19); (2) *a forgiving God*—"We have sinned against thee" (14:20); (3) *an honor-preserving throne*—"Do not disgrace the throne of thy glory: remember, break not thy covenant with us" (14:21); (4) *an omnipotent Creator*—"We will wait for thee" to bring rain and showers, "for thou hast made all these things" (14:22).

And Jeremiah would have waited for God to send the rain, persevering and long-suffering prophet that he was. If only time had been the sole obstacle!

4. *From Despondency to Hope: Jeremiah As the Rejected Intercessor* (15:1-21).[33]

In the final intercessory prayer (14:19-22), Jeremiah

_____
[33]Paragraphs at 1,5,10,11,15,19.

had reached a pitch of almost desperate intensity. Chapter 15 records the sequel to this priestly appeal to God, showing a despondent servant and the hopeful words of his Master.

a. Despondency (15:1-10). Like poured water on glowing ashes, God's response to Jeremiah's plea fell with abrupt finality: No amount of intercession would be heard for the people—not even if the great intercessors Moses and Samuel should speak (15:1)—for it was not now the hour of intercession; rather, the day of doom had arrived. The prophet's unpopular task was to preach death, sword, famine, and captivity (15:2), in accordance with the designed appointments of God (15:3). The sins of Manasseh, multiplied manifold in the second and third generations thereafter, were beginning to take their toll.

The prophet, forced to step out of the role of intercessor for the time being, looked on his people in compassion and bemoaned the fact that they had none to pity them (15:5).[34] But God's words to them tell why they should not have had pity: they had rejected Him, and therefore had begun to reap judgment already (15:6-9; notice the repetition of "I have"). This brought the prophet to one of the lowest points of his prophetic career. He despaired of life itself: "Woe is me, my mother, that thou hast borne me. . ." (15:10). He was a friendless, discouraged, and frustrated man, but God had not forsaken him.

b. Hope (15:11-21). Lifting Jeremiah out of the slough of despond, God promised him that good would eventual-

---

[34]Some expositors take 15:5 to be the words of Jehovah. The context would allow this, but the more natural reading would assign the words to Jeremiah, with God beginning to speak again at 15:6-9.

ly come out of the seemingly hopeless situation of ever-present enemies, trials, tribulation (15:11) and a doomed nation, Judah (15:12-14). Jeremiah began to revive his spirit again (15:15-16), although he had not yet fully found an answer to the perpetual pain which he experienced as a prophet to his people (15:18).

God then made hope shine in all its splendor for the prophet (15:19-21). If the prophet would return in heart to the place of trusting God's wisdom and love (15:19), victory and blessing would be his reward. The antidote for the prophet's earlier "Woe is me" was the Lord's "I am with thee" (15:20). No better word could ever be given by God to one of His servants, anywhere or anytime! The words of the prophecy that followed show more of the blessed efficacy of the divine promises.

Are there intercessors like Jeremiah in the world today? Are there Christian men and women who intimately *feel* the desperate plight of lost souls, who must unceasingly cry to God on their behalf for His mercy and forgiveness, who are assured that nothing is impossible wth God, and who rest their own souls in the blessed confidence of the eternal Saviour who redeemed them? Vacant places of intercession plead today for occupation.

5. *In This Place: Jeremiah Alone in a Punished Place* (16:1-18).[35]

Jeremiah could not have felt the gnawing pain of utter loneliness more intensely than when he heard God speak these words to him. In deep despair, he had wished he had never been born into this unpopular plight of a hated prophet (15:10). Then the loneliness of it all was etched

[35]Paragraphs at 1,5,10,14,16.

across his already bleeding heart. Of all the places in the vast universe, why had God put him *in this place?*

a. Grievous Family Deaths (16:1-4). In this place, said God, would come grievous deaths of entire families with no burials because of the mass of corpses. Jeremiah was commanded not to marry here,[36] and therefore not to have children, in order to be spared the future sorrow of a bereaved husband and father. Nevertheless he could not escape the hurt of the solitary life demanded thereby.

b. No Mourning or Mirth (16:5-9). The soul-satisfaction that comes to the spiritual shepherd of a flock in ministering to their grief was denied the prophet in this case, not because God would withhold blessing from His faithful servant but because the judgment to come would be sudden, short, total, and without opportunity for a shepherd's service. When that judgment was to come, tender mercies would have been taken away (16:5), with no hour for mourning (16:6-7) or mirth (16:8-9). In that day, Jeremiah was to stand aloof, not able to serve.

c. Worse Evil (16:10-13). Jehovah revealed to Jeremiah that when the foregoing message of judgment was delivered to the people, their reaction would be, "Why?. . . What crime have we done?" (16:10). Jeremiah was then to answer for God, "Because your fathers have forsaken me. . . and ye have done evil more than your fathers" (16:11-12). Here the prophet had to stand as a lone voice, spokesman for the Great Judge.

d. Surrender to Bondage (16:14-15). The Babylonian captivity would be so critical an experience in the history of Judah that it would alter for the centuries to come

---

[36]There was no prohibition to marry after the judgment days were over, however.

the Jews' testimony concerning God's deliverance. The land of Canaan, until the time of this judgment, had been known as the place to which God brought the Israelites from Egypt (16:14); whereas, in the post-captivity days, it would be known as the place to which God regathered His people *from the North* "and from *all the countries* whither He had driven them" (16:15). This geographical reference suggests an application with reference to the final regathering of Israel in the last days. The implied tone of the paragraph is that of judgment, although the prospect of eventual restoration or return is clearly stated. Anathoth, Jerusalem, the hills and valleys of Judea, all the sentimental places of Jeremiah's lifetime, were to be surrendered, and the prophet would be compelled to take on the lonely role of a prophet without a country.

e. No Escapees (16:16-18). Trying to hide from God by seeking hiding places in mountains and hills, in clefts of rocks, and in rivers and seas, would be futile for the people of Judah, for God was to send, as it were, fishermen and hunters to search out all the guilty from their hiding places to bring them to their double recompense. The place of sin is the place of judgment, never a place of hiding. "For mine eyes are upon all their ways. . . neither is their iniquity concealed from mine eyes" (16:17).

The picture of the lonely prophet is now complete, for the people had gone into judgment, and the prophet walked alone.

6. *The Heart: Jeremiah Remains True in Heart* (16:19—17:18)[37]

The central core of teaching in this segment of

---
[37]Paragraphs at 16:19; 17:1,5,9,12.

Jeremiah's prophecy is found in 17:5-11, the two paragraphs of which stand out in the context because of (1) the omission of local, provincial truths, such as specific sins and judgments of the specific nation, Judah, and (2) the presence of universal truths about the heart of man. This commentary commences at this central core, and then analyzes the surrounding paragraphs.

a. What the Heart Is by Nature (17:9-11). Very succinctly the doctrine is stated that the heart is exceedingly deceitful and corrupt, is known fully only by God, and is the source and determinant of the spiritual fruits of a man's life (17:9-10). This latter law of recompense is illustrated by the man who obtains riches wrongfully, and ends up as a fool (17:11).

b. What the Heart May Choose (17:5-8). Man was created not as a mechanical robot but as a person with a will, with the power of choice. Two basic options always face him: the good and the evil. The evil choice is that of self-confidence and therefore self-righteousness, in which the heart departs from God and is therefore cursed in parched desert living (17:5-6). The good choice is trusting in God, for which there is blessed, fruitful, and healthy spiritual living (17:7-8).

c. Examples of the Good and Evil Choices. The surrounding context cites examples of both choices made by nations and individuals:

1) Heathen Nations (16:19-21). At some future time unspecified by the prophet there would be a day when non-Israelite nations would come to God and confess their idolatry (16:19-20). For this act of repentance God would give them knowledge of Himself—both of His power ("my hand and my might") and of His person

57

("and they shall know that my name is Jehovah," 16:21).
2) Judah (17:1-4). In contrast to the righteous
option to be chosen by Gentile nations, Judah had pre-
ferred the evil way. Her sin was written with a pen of iron,
and with the point of a diamond" (17:1). For her idolatry,
a fire in God's anger had been kindled to burn forever,
and Judah was to serve her enemies in a strange land
(17:2-4).
3) Jeremiah and his persecutors (17:12-18). Even
as the bright paragraph of 16:19-21 was introduced with
an ascription of trust ("O Jehovah, my strength, and my
stronghold, and my refuge in the day of affliction. . .,"
16:19), so this predominantly bright paragraph is introduced with a similar ascription: "A glorious throne, set
on high from the beginning, is the place of our sanctuary"
(17:12). Jeremiah asked for deliverance for himself (17:
14, 17a, 18). He also declared his trust in Jehovah:
"Thou art my refuge in the day of evil" (17:17b). His
persecutors, on the other hand, had chosen the evil path,
their persecution of him being traceable back to their forsaking Jehovah, and their future being destined for double
destruction (17:13, 18).

Thus the prophet had risen from the slough of despondency to the height of personal, tried trust in Jehovah,
his warm intercessory heart reconciled to the punitive
judgments of a God who cannot dwell with shame!

7. *The Law of the Sabbath*: *Jeremiah Preaches at
the City's Gates* (17:19-27)[38]

This Sabbath-day sermon was preached at some time
during Jehoiakim's reign, though not necessarily in connection with the message of the preceding section, 16:19—

---

[38]Paragraphs at 19,24.

17:18. Its teaching, however, is pertinent to the heart emphasis of that message, and its location at this point in the book is therefore appropriate.

The real test of the heart's relation to God is *obedience to His Word*. One of the laws for Israel was the hallowing of the Sabbath by not working on that day (17: 21-22). The constant pressure of materialism upon the lives of all, including the people of God, made the keeping of such a commandment difficult, and for this reason this one commandment of the ten was a real test of the priority of the temporal or the eternal in the heart. Was the keeping of the Sabbath law that crucial to Judah? The symbolic action of Jeremiah and the explicit words he was told to speak gave an affirmative answer:

a. The action. Jeremiah was to "stand in the gate . . . whereby the kings of Judah come in, and by which they go out" (17:19), denoting that his message related to the very peace of the city and the prosperity of its throne.

b. The words. If the people hallowed the Sabbath, "then shall there enter in by the gates of this city kings and princes sitting upon the throne of David. . . and this city shall remain for ever" (17:25). For disobeying, the gates and palaces would be devoured (17:27).

God had reasons for instituting a day of rest (Sabbath) for Israel, even as the same principles today underlie the day of rest (Lord's Day) for the Church. The Sabbath was for physical and spiritual refreshment and recharging (Deut. 5:14), remembrance of divine redemption (Deut. 5:15), and magnification of the Lord as consecrator (Exodus 31:13). The Christian today is to observe the Lord's Day in the same spirit, recognizing it as a memorial

59

of the glorious event of Christ's resurrection on the first day of the week.

8. *Lessons from Pottery: Jeremiah Learns and Preaches from Pottery* (18:1—20:18)[39]

These three chapters form a fitting conclusion to the Discourses (Book I) of Jeremiah's prophecy. Very impressively they summarize the thrust of the previous chapters and bring to a climax the published messages and experiences of the prophet during the reign of Jehoiakim.

God spoke to Jeremiah and the people by way of two symbols of pottery. The account of the first symbol reiterates the long-suffering of God (chap. 18); the second describes the judgment of God (19:1—20:6). The following sequence of description is given each symbol: the symbol, the message, the response, and the prophet's involvement and plea.

a. The Symbol of Long-suffering (18:1-23). The symbol was not a single item but a total picture seen by the prophet in the potter's house.[40] As the potter was making a vessel on the wheels,[41] it became marred or misformed in his hand, but he did not throw it away. Instead, while it was still in a moldable stage, "he made it again another vessel," a good one (18:1-4).

The symbol was clear enough. God's interpretation of it left no doubt as to its message: (1) He was sovereign over Israel—"as clay in the potter's hand, so are ye in my hand" (18:6). This sovereignty extended to judgment

---

[39]Paragraphs at 18:1,5,13,18,19; 19:1,10,14; 20:1,7,14.

[40]The potter's house was probably located in the "potter's field," which was just beyond the Valley of Hinnom, south of Jerusalem.

[41]The wheels were two circular stones connected by a vertical shaft. The lower wheel was turned by the feet, engaging the upper wheel to its circular motion, where the potter, with two free hands, formed the vessel from a lump of clay.

("pluck up," 18:7) or blessing ("build," 18:9). (2) His sovereignty did not preclude the free will of man to choose righteousness ("turn from their evil," 18:8) or sin ("obey not my voice," 18:10). Judgment or blessing pronounced by God at the beginning could be reversed or confirmed before being sealed, depending on Israel's heart choice in the day of extended grace.[42] (3) Israel, though judgment had been pronounced, still lived in the day of extended grace, for she was invited to *"return. . . and amend"* her ways (18:11).

But the symbol of the marred vessel was not given to leave the invitation to return as a last word to the Israelites. They had already been given that invitation (cf. 3:1—4:4), and they had refused it. The symbol begins with the idea of invitation in order to present the sequels: (1) the declination of the invitation ("But they say. . . we will walk after our own devices," 18:12), (2) the horribleness of the sin (18:13-16), and (3) the already pronounced judgment, "I will scatter them as with an east wind before the enemy" (18:17).

We are to assume that Jeremiah preached to the people the lessons of the marred vessel, for the account tells us of their heated conspiracy against the prophet. They would "smite him with the tongue," castigating him as an unnecessary and undesirable member of their order and society (18:18), dig a pit for his soul (18:19,22), hide snares for his feet (18:22), and slay him (18:23). The prophet, however, rested his case with God in an impreca-

---

[42]Notice the similarity of God's relation to Israel and His relation to the human race today. Every individual is born a guilty sinner, already under condemnation. However, the judgment of condemnation can be reversed in this lifetime, depending on the individual's heart choice to believe on Christ.

61

tory prayer for *His* vengeance upon his enemies for their contentions (18:19-23).

b. The Symbol of Judgment (19:1—20:6). The second symbol of the potter's earthen bottle was given to extend the message of the marred vessel. The first symbol taught the sovereignty and long-suffering of God, the invitation of a second chance, and its rejection and consequence. The earthen bottle episode taught the awfulness and irreversibility of the impending judgment.

The prophet was commanded to buy a potter's earthen bottle and go to the Valley of Hinnom with elders of the people and elders of the priests and preach a message directed to the kings of Judah and inhabitants of Jerusalem (19:1-3). The earthen bottle itself would be used as an object lesson after Jeremiah had finished speaking of Israel's idolatrous sin (introduced by "because," 19:4-5) and the catastrophic consequences (introduced by "therefore," 19:6-9). At this point Jeremiah was to break the bottle in the sight of the men with him, and deliver the message of the symbol: "Even so will I break this people and this city, as one breaketh a potter's vessel, *that cannot be made whole again*" (19:11). There is no message of remolding a marred vessel here. The earthen vessel was irrevocably destroyed. The application to Judah was all too obvious.

Going from Topheth to the court of the temple, Jeremiah repeated the message of imminent doom for Jerusalem and all its environs (19:14-15). Pashhur, the chief officer of the temple, heard Jeremiah prophesy, and struck him and imprisoned him (20:1-2). Released the next morning, Jeremiah pronounced two very explicit divine judgments (20:3-6). The first was against the man Pashhur—one of the relatively few judgments against individual persons recorded in the book. Pashhur's name was changed to Magor-missabib ("Terror on every side"), for he would be a terror to himself and to all his friends, to whom he had prophesied falsely (20:4,6). The second prophecy of judgment was against the nation Judah. Here, for the first time in the prophecy, the king of Babylon is explicitly identified as the conqueror of Judah (20:4-5). Up to this time the conqueror had been identified as the enemy from the North. Now, inspired to speak the explicit prophecy uttered by Isaiah a century before,[43] Jeremiah exposed the enemy by name. And for those who lightly passed off the threat of Babylon, there would come the shameful day of death in that very land. Pashhur was such a person (20:6).

The confessions and reflections of Jeremiah as recorded in 20:7-18 may be read as the conclusion of the earthen bottle story alone, or as the conclusion to the section as a whole (18:1—20:18). In the first paragraph (18:7-13) all shades of the prophet's emotions, intellect, and will are seen. He traced his prophetic ministry back to the overpowering[44] voice of God (20:7). True to that voice, he had shouted the message, "Violence and destruction!" But for this he had been made a laughingstock, a reproach,

---

[43]Isaiah 39:6-7.

[44]The Hebrew word for "persuade" does not have in it the idea of befooling or enticing, as suggested by the marginal note of the American Standard Version. Carl F. Keil says the word "does not mean befool, but persuade, induce by words to do a thing." Carl F. Keil, and Franz J. Delitzsch, *The Prophecies of Jeremiah* (Grand Rapids: Wm. B. Eerdmans Publishing Co., 1950), I, 316. However, the word is translated "deceived" by the AV and RSV, "enticed" by the Jewish Publications Society translation (*The Holy Scriptures: According to the Masoretic Text* [Cleveland: World Publishing Co., n.d.], for the Jewish Publications Society).

and a derision continually. Whenever he had rationalized that it woud be more pleasant for him not to speak of Jehovah, there was as it were a "burning fire shut up" in his "bones" (20:9). He *had* to speak the message of God. And, thus speaking, he also had to be willing to see all his familiar friends turn against him, seeking revenge (20:10). But the fact that *God was with him* more than compensated for separation from friends (20:11). Recognizing that he was thus associated with One so mighty and terrible, just and righteous, the prophet rises at the end of his reflections to the acme of praise: "Sing unto Jehovah, praise ye Jehovah . . ." (20:13).

Jeremiah's wail of despair recorded in the paragraph that follows (20:14-18) is in bold contrast to the song of praise in the foregoing paragraph. By its very nature it could not have been spoken by the prophet immediately after the reflections of 20:7-13. Its position in the scroll of the prophet, however, may be accepted as authentic for the simple reason that the song of 20:13 had not driven away, once and for all, the tempter of despair. Jeremiah had yet to experience more of the dark hours. In one sense they would be darker hours, climaxed eventually in the hour of his beloved city's destruction. Somewhere, he gave in to the darkness for a time, and cursed the day of his birth (20:14-18). But this was only temporary. When Jerusalem finally fell, the prophet did not fall with her. For the years of trials had molded this lonely, forsaken servant of God to be stronger, more courageous, and more compassionate. The most extreme test was no match for his complete trust in God. May the same be true of God's servants today!

BOOK TWO

(Chapters 21-44)

I. LATER PROPHECIES (21:1—33:26)

   A.   The Sure Captivity (21:1—29:32)
       1. The Decreed Judgments (21:11—25:38)
       2. The Authorized Prophet (26:1—29:32)

   B.   The Ultimate Deliverance (30:1—33:26)
       1. A Returned People (30:1—31:26)
       2. A Complete Renovation (31:27-40)
       3. The Test of Faith (32:1—33:26)

II. DAYS OF FULFILLMENT (34:1—44:30)

   A.   The Siege of Jerusalem (34:1—38:28)
       1. Outcome of the Siege Restated (34:1-7)
       2. Sin of the People Renewed (34:8—35:19)
       3. The Prophet of God Apprehended
          (36:1—38:28)

   B.   The Fall of Jerusalem (39:1-18)
       1. The Toll (39:4-10)
       2. Two Men Delivered (39:11-18)

   C.   Events in Judah After Jerusalem's Fall
      (40:1—44:30)
       1. Governorship of Gedaliah (40:1—41:18)
       2. Migration to Egypt (42:1—43:7)
       3. Judgment of the Refugees (43:8—44:30)

I. LATER PROPHECIES (21:1—33:26)

FOLLOWING A GENERAL PATTERN of chronology, the book
of Jeremiah now records messages and experiences of the
prophet on the eve of the fall of Jerusalem. The prophet's
message and the entire book of Jeremiah revolve about
this critical event. As previously shown, the chapters of
Book One are related to the reigns of Josiah and Jehoiakim, in that order. Most of the chapters[1] of Book Two
are dated in the reign of Zedekiah, successor to Jehoiakim
after the very brief intervening reign of Jehoiachin. Zedekiah was the last of Judah's kings before Jerusalem fell.[2]

When Nebuchadnezzar's armies invaded Judah in 597,
they took King Jehoiachin captive along with ten thousand
of the best people of the land. Mattaniah, youngest son of
Josiah, was placed on the throne, and his name was
changed by Nebuchadnezzar to Zedekiah (meaning literally "Jehovah is my righteousness"). He was placed on
the throne by the very nation that incarcerated him eleven
years later.

If the Babylonian king hoped for something good in
such a relationship to Judah, he was soon utterly disillu-
sioned. Zedekiah, loyal to Nebuchadnezzar in word only,
made secret alliances with surrounding nations and eventually revolted against Babylon. This was the *political, international* cause for the Babylonian invasion against
Judah in the ninth year of Zedekiah's reign, bringing Jerusalem's fall. The *basic, spiritual* causes are the subject of
the entire book of Jeremiah.

---

[1] Of this section (chaps. 21-33), chapters 25 and 26 are probably
dated in Jehoiakim's reign, but inserted in the middle of the Zedekiah chapters because of what they contribute topically to the
surrounding context.

[2] The biblical historical background to the reign of Zedekiah is
given in II Kings 24:18—25:30 and II Chronicles 36:11-23.

The holy city's destruction was at hand, and the Prophet Jeremiah was engaged by God to say more about the causes and judgments of God's "holy wars" against rebellious men and nations. Chapters 21 through 29 tell of the sure captivity, followed by the brightest section in the entire prophecy, Jeremiah's *evangelium* of the New Covenant (chaps. 30-33).

A. The Sure Captivity (21:1—29:32)

The fall of Jerusalem was sure and inevitable because the judgment had been decreed by God (21:1—25:38) and announced to the people by a divinely authorized prophet, Jeremiah (26:7—29:32).

At one point during the siege of Jerusalem, which lasted about eighteen months, Zedekiah sent two emissaries to Jeremiah asking him to inquire of Jehovah whether He would favor Judah and cause Nebuchadnezzar to retreat. The answer of Jehovah was an unequivocal no. He Himself would fight against Judah (21:5), delivering the survivors of the battle into the hands of Nebuchadnezzar (21:3-7). The people had to submit to this divinely programmed judgment of captivity to the Chaldeans or forfeit their own lives (21:8-10).

1. *The Decreed Judgments* (21:11—25:38)

The judgments of God were spelled out more clearly than ever before. They reached to Judah's kings, prophets, and people, and included Babylon and the other ungodly foreign nations as well.

a. Against Kings (21:11—23:8). The general indictment against Judah's kings is introduced in the first two paragraphs (21:11—22:9).[3] Both paragraphs contain sim-

---

[3]Though the two paragraphs may have been originally written at two different times, contiguity and similarity of content justify their being studied together.

ilar references to the throne: "hour of the king of Judah"; "throne of David"; "execute justice." The "lest" of 21:12 and the "if" of 22:5 are not intended to be interpreted that the fall of Jerusalem was at this hour of Zedekiah's reign still conditional. Rather, the conditions of righteousness (22:3) and obedience (22:5) were stated to reiterate the areas of violation and the causes of the judgment: "Thou art Gilead unto me, and the head of Lebanon; yet surely I will make thee a wilderness, and cities which are not inhabited" (22:6).

Three kings of Judah were singled out as reaping the judgment of God.[4] Since each of the three consecutive kings listed (Shallum, or Jehoahaz, 22:11; Jehoiakim, 22:18; and Coniah, or Jehoiachin, 22:24) were predecessors of Zedekiah, he could have learned from their experiences, and the concentration of the three messages at this place in Jeremiah could very well have been to focus attention on the light which Zedekiah had.[5]

1) King Shallum, or Jehoahaz,[6] was to die as a captive in a foreign land, which subsequent history showed to be

---

[4]See Appendix II for background on the kings of Judah.

[5]It is difficult to say when each of the three messages was originally delivered. There is good support for the view that all three were delivered during the reign of Jehoiakim (cf. 22:11 and 22:24a). Another view is that the prophet delivered them separately during the respective reigns of the kings and that shortly after Zedekiah's enthronement Jeremiah's scribe brought the three oracles together on a scroll and delivered it to the King as exemplary warning to him. (See Howard T. Kuist, "The Book of Jeremiah," *Interpretation,* July, 1950, p. 332.) Whatever the case, all three oracles were a matter of record by the time Zedekiah came to the throne.

[6]II Kings 23:30. Cf. I Chronicles 3:15. "The dead" of Jeremiah 22:10a probably refers to Josiah.

Egypt.[7] Jehoahaz' epitaph of shame was "He shall see this land [Judah] no more" (22:10-12).

2) The second example to Zedekiah was the king succeeding Shallum, Jehoiakim, who also had been warned of judgment to come. Jeremiah's denunciation of Jehoiakim was vehement. This king had built a beautiful palace but had also plundered his people in unjust ways, including forced labor. His concept of respected royalty was in terms of palatial show. His father Josiah had left an enviable record of righteousness and care for the poor and needy; but Jehoiakim looked only to covetousness, murder, oppression, and violence (22:15-17). His end was not to be the respectful burial of a hero or friend, but one reflecting the course of his reign: he was to be buried "with the burial of an ass, drawn and cast forth beyond the gates of Jerusalem" (22:18-19).

3) The third king who served as an example to Zedekiah was Coniah, or Jehoiachin.[8] The description of his judgment was prefixed by a call to the people of Judah to mourn for their kings ("lovers")[9] who had been condemned to captivity (22:20-23). Their cry of mourning was to be loud (from the high peaks of Lebanon to the north, Bashan to the northeast, and Abarim to the southeast, (22:20), because they were "greatly to be pitied" (22:23). Jehoiachin, Zedekiah's immediate predecessor, had been told that he and his mother would be taken captive to Babylon, where he would die childless; that is,

---

[7]II Kings 23:34.

[8]See II Kings 24:6,8.

[9]The "lovers" are interpreted by Keil and Delitzsch as being the surrounding nations. Carl F. Keil and Franz J. Delitzsch, *The Prophecies of Jeremiah* (Grand Rapids: Wm. B. Eerdmans Publishing Co., 1950), II, 342.

he would have no *reigning* children "sitting upon the throne of David" (22:25-30).[10]

The kings as national sovereigns had exerted tremendous sway in leading their people astray, scattering the sheep of God's pasture (23:1-2). Yet, God was to make the ultimate dispositions of fate, which included the regathering of some of His people back to the land of promise. The bold contrast is stated by God thus: "Ye have scattered. . . . I will gather" (23:2-3). The first fulfillment of this was the return of the remnant to Canaan after the time of captivity, to dwell prosperously and safely, and to be ruled by a righteous and just throne (23:3-5). History has shown that restoration to be a temporary flicker of light, for by the time of Malachi (the last of the prophets, *c*. 400 B.C.), Israel had degenerated again to a people with stony hearts.

The second fulfillment, though more distant, was to outshine the first in splendor and glory. The "righteous Branch" of David[11] would be the Messiah, called by the name "Jehovah our righteousness" (23:5-6). In the last days He would gather together the remnant of Israel from all the countries whither He had driven them, to bring

---

[10]Actually, Jehoiachin had seven sons (I Chron. 3:17-18), of whom Shealtiel is listed in the genealogy of Jesus in Matthew 1:12. This is no contradiction of Jeremiah's prophecy, however, for Matthew's record of David's lineage indicates only that Joseph, descended from Shealtiel, was Jesus' *legal* father, in the sense that he was Mary's husband. The Gospel is very careful in its recording of the birth of Jesus as to his *real* Father. While "begat" is the usual term applied to the *real* father (or grandfather, etc.), in the genealogical list, the same word is avoided in the case of Joseph: "and Jacob begat Joseph the husband of Mary, of whom was born Jesus, who is called Christ" (Matt. 1:16). Also, Joseph was clearly told by an angel that that which was conceived in Mary was "of the Holy Spirit" (Matt. 1:20). So, no man of Jehoiachin's seed sat upon the throne of David!

[11]Cf. 33:15.

them to dwell in their own land (23:8). Thereafter the memorial of His people would not commemorate deliverance from Egypt, but deliverance from bondage in the world (23:7).

The rebuke brought against the line of kings, including the contemporary King Zedekiah, closes in a touch of irony. Zedekiah, whose name literally means "Jehovah is my righteousness," had betrayed his calling. The righteous Branch, "Jehovah our righteousness,"—Jesus—must come to salvage the ruins.

b. Against Prophets (23:9-40). "Behold, I am against the prophets" (23:30). The indictment against the prophets was severe, but justly so. God had seen folly in the prophets of Samaria, the land of the Northern Kingdom, and He had seen nothing but ungodliness in the prophets of Jerusalem, representing the land of the Southern Kingdom (23:9-15). The false prophets had taught lies, refusing to stand in the council of God to know His words (23:16-22). They had claimed to have contact with a secret otherworld through dreams (23:23-32), refusing thereby (1) to acknowledge that God is omnipresent, filling heaven and earth (there is no secret otherworld) (23:23-24), and (2) to distinguish between God's words and a man's dream: "The prophet that hath a dream, let him tell a dream; and he that hath my word, let him speak my word faithfully" (23:28).

The words of 23:33-40 expand on the truth of point 2 above. When the people had asked, "What is the oracle?" the prophets had answered with their own words, representing them as though coming from divine source (23:34,36*b*). Therefore God commanded the prophets not to mention the oracle of Jehovah anymore (23:36),

71

so that the people would not be deceived about the source of the message.

There is an interesting play on the key word, *oracle,* of 23:33-40, translated "burden" in the American Standard Version. The Hebrew word is *massa,* which has a dual usage. Meaning "lifted" or "taken up," it can be translated "oracle" (taken up on the lips) or "burden" (e.g., taken up on the shoulder). When the people asked, "What is the burden [*massa,* oracle] of Jehovah?" then the word of Jehovah was "You are the [*massa*] burden! And I will cast you off" (Berkeley Version, 23:33).

c. Against Zedekiah (24:1-10). Topically, this chapter could have been placed after the section describing God's judgments of the kings (21:11—23:8), for it continues that prophecy by foretelling the destiny of the last and contemporary king, Zedekiah.[12] In other words, the section of the judgments against kings is broken into, in a sense, by the section of the judgments against prophets (23:9-40). It is very likely that chapter 24 was kept out of the sequence of chapters 21 through 23 because of its difference in style[13] (parable) and because its message came to Jeremiah at an earlier date.[14]

At the beginning of Zedekiah's reign, after Nebuchadnezzar had taken Jehoiachin and a host of Israelites captive, Jehovah showed Jeremiah two baskets of figs set before the temple. One basket had very good figs; the other, very bad figs (24:1-3). God interpreted the good figs to represent His ultimate favorable disposition of the

[12]The paragraph 24:4-7, regarding restoration, is also very similar to 23:3-8.

[13]Philip Schaff (ed.), "Jeremiah," *Lange's Commentary on the Holy Scriptures* (Grand Rapids: Zondervan Pub. House, n.d.), 6, 193.

[14]As also the message of chapter 25.

captives of Judah who were sent into the land of the Chaldeans. Physically, they would be brought back to Canaan and built up (24:6). Spiritually, He would give them a heart to return to Him, to know Him as Jehovah (24:7).

The bad figs represented what God would ultimately do to Zedekiah and the residue of Judah who remained in the land. The king and his people would be "tossed to and fro among all the kingdoms of the earth for evil; to be a reproach, and a proverb, a taunt, and a curse. . ." (24:8-9).

d. Against the People (25:1-11). No prophets, priests, princes, or kings are mentioned here. The section is directed solely to "all the people of Judah" (25:1). The prophecy came to Jeremiah in his twenty-third year as a prophet to the people (25:3). It was the accession year of Nebuchadnezzar. The Battle of Carchemish (on the Euphrates in Syria, 605 B.C.) had just ended; Nebuchadnezzar had defeated Neco II of Egypt and destroyed Egyptian power in Asia (II Chron. 35:20; Jer. 46:2).

The indictment against the people is cutting. God had spoken to the people through His prophets, Jeremiah included, for many years (e.g., the twenty-three years of Jeremiah's preaching). He had taken the initiative and had been more anxious to save the people than they had been to be saved (God's "rising up early," 25:4). The essence of His warning and invitation had been "Return ye now every one from his evil way" (25:5). Yet the people did not hearken, and so had to face captivity under Nebuchadnezzar (25:8).

It is at this point in the book of Jeremiah that the duration of the captivity is first mentioned. The king of Babylon was to be served seventy years dating from the time of the prophecy, 605 B.C.[15]

e. Against Babylon (25:12-14). After the seventy years had been accomplished, Jehovah would punish Nebuchadnezzar and his nation "for their iniquity," revealing again that they were not chosen to be Judah's conquerors for any righteous merit of their own, but rather by the sovereign design of God.

f. Against Other Nations (25:15-38). Babylon was not the only foreign nation destined for judgment. Jehovah had a controversy with *all* the nations (25:31). The interesting observation to be made about these twenty-four verses is that there is no explicit reference to the sin of the nations; the entire section describes only their judgment. One clue is given, however, as to the key sin. This is found in 25:29: "For, lo, I begin to work evil at the city which is called by my name; and should *ye* be utterly unpunished? . . ."[16] God was about to destroy *His own* holy city and punish *His own* people for sin. That the nations were also deserving of punishment implies that they were at least as guilty of sin as the people of Judah. That sin, although not stated in this section, was, of course, *idolatry*.

That Jeremiah's prophetic ministry extended even to foreign nations is clearly demonstrated here, where the prophet was commanded symbolically to cause all the nations to drink God's cup of the wine of wrath. The nations are listed in 25:18-26. The truth of God's sovereignty over *all* nations is emphasized by repetition thus:

---

[15]The number 70 is a round number if the period ran from 605 B.C. to 538 B.C., the year of Cyrus' decree permitting the exiles' return (an interval of 67 years). Some reckon the dating from the destruction of the temple, 586 B.C. to the completion of the temple's reconstruction, 516 B.C.

[16]Italics mine.

"For I will call for a sword upon all the inhabitants of the earth" (25:29), "against all the inhabitants of the earth" (25:30), "from the uttermost parts of the earth" (25:32), and "from one end of the earth even unto the other end of the earth" (25:33). The progression of description of judgment from local nations to all the kingdoms of the world has the impact of recognizing God's sovereignty with respect to not only place but also time, prophesying as it were even unto the end times, the "great day of God," when kings of the whole world will be gathered to Har-Magedon (Armageddon) for His judgment (Rev. 16:14-16).

This section identifying the judgments of God against the evil nations is expanded in chapters 46 through 51.[17] These chapters are appropriately held off until the end of the book of Jeremiah since the main burden of the prophet is the destiny of his own people, Judah, and the record would therefore give precedence to this. Furthermore, the judgments upon the evil nations would fall after the judgment upon Judah, and so the position of chapters 46 through 51 is chronologically fitting at the end of the book. Jeremiah justifiably included the smaller section of judgment against foreign nations (25:15-38) in the middle of the book, for he desired to record, on the eve of the fall of Jerusalem, the pertinent judgments of God against *all* the main groups involved: kings, prophets, the people, Babylon, and the evil nations.

* * *

What of ungodly nations today, in this age of deification of science and man? Are such nations impregnable? The

---

[17]The similarity of both sections is recognized by the Septuagint Version in placing the content of chapters 46 through 51 between 25:13 and 25:14 of our versions.

prophet's words of millennia ago concerning the finality of God's judgments are as pertinent today as then: "And thou shalt say unto them [the nations], Thus saith Jehovah of hosts, the God of Israel: Drink ye, and be drunken, and spew, and fall, and rise no more. . ." (25:27).

2. *The Authorized Prophet* (26:1—29:32)

The subject of the previous five chapters has been the certainty of judgment to come. In the next four chapters attention is directed to the man Jeremiah, who preached the message of judgment. The captivity had been shown to be certain by the fact of the irrevocable decree of a sovereign God (chaps. 21-25). Now it was shown to be certain by the fact of the divine authority attending the prophet chosen to declare it.

a. Jeremiah's Life Spared (26:1-24). Reaching back to the time of the beginning of Jehoiakim's reign, Jeremiah's record brings to light the story attending his "Temple Discourse," the words of which are recorded in chapters 7 through 10. The story is very pertinent at this point because the prophet's own experiences confirm the authenticity of his message. The Apostle Paul defended his divine authority in the same manner in writing his epistle to the Galatians.

The temple sermon which Jeremiah had been commanded to deliver "in the court of Jehovah's house" is represented in condensed form by only one sentence in this chapter (26:4-6), since the burden of the chapter is to report the reactions to the message rather than the total sum of the words themselves. The essence of his message is the warning that he gave from God that if the people did not hearken to God, their holy temple and city would be made a curse before all nations. Jeremiah had delivered the sermon to an audience comprised of priests, prophets, and all the people (26:7). Their reaction was violent. "Thou shalt surely die!" they screamed (26:8). They charged Jeremiah with pronouncing, in the name of Jehovah, doom on the holy temple and holy city (26:9). To them, Jeremiah was guilty of blasphemy.

The trial of the prophet took place before the princes at the entry of the new gate of the temple (26:10). The priests and prophets accused him before the princes and all the people. Then Jeremiah was permitted to state his defense (26:12-15). It is a classic for its conciseness, frankness, and courage:

1) *Authority*—"Jehovah sent me" (26:12).
2) *Message of Warning*—"to prophesy against this house" (26:12).
3) *Message of Invitation*—"amend your ways . . . and obey the voice of Jehovah" (26:13).
4) *Committal*—"do with me [my body] as is good and right in your eyes" (26:14). Jeremiah knew, however, that they could not touch his soul.
5) *Warning*—"if ye put me to death, ye will bring innocent blood upon yourselves" (26:15).
6) *Authority*—"for of a truth Jehovah hath sent me unto you to speak all these words in your ears" (26:15). As Jeremiah's defense had opened with a statement of authority, so it closed with the same note.

The verdict of the princes and the people was prompt and overwhelming: "this man is not worthy of death" (26:16). Having recognized the prophet's authority, they gave as the reason for the verdict that Jeremiah had spoken unto them truly in the name of Jehovah (26:16). The verdict was shared by certain of the elders who recalled that King Hezekiah almost a century earlier did not slay the Prophet Micah for prophesying this message: "Zion shall be plowed as a field, and Jerusalem shall become heaps, and the mountain of the house as the high places of the forest" (26:17-19; Micah 3:12). The interesting observation here is that while the people and the princes recognized Jeremiah's divine authority, they apparently still refused to amend their ways and obey God's voice, or this would have been the beginning of spiritual awakening in the nation, a change which Jeremiah longed to see.

The concluding paragraph, 26:20-24, is interesting for what it teaches and what it does not teach. It does *not* teach that a prophet of God is assured total immunity from a martyr's death, or death for a witness. Thus Uriah, who prophesied in the name of Jehovah a message very similar to Jeremiah's, was eventually slain by King Jehoiakim, and his body was cast into the cemetery of the common people (26:20-23). One can explain Uriah's martyrdom in the light of that which the record proceeds to tell concerning the experience of Jeremiah. Here in the last verse of the chapter we learn that death to God's servants comes only in God's time when the prophets' work is done. As for Uriah, it was assuredly God's time to receive him. We know this was not so for Jeremiah, for God had told him that he would live to see the fall of the holy city. Death therefore could not touch him prematurely. And so God used Ahikam, father of Gedaliah (governor of Jerusalem after its fall), to protect Jeremiah from being given "into the hand of the people to put him to death" (26:24).

b. Jeremiah's Message Authenticated (27:1—29:32). Chapters 27 and 28, describing events which took place in the fourth year of Zedekiah's reign,[18] confirm the divine authority of the Prophet Jeremiah in his confrontation with the false prophets who were denying his message.

The explosive byword of Jeremiah's prophecy at this time was "Serve Babylon and live" (27:11,12,17). As viewed by the prophets and the people, such a word was inconsistent with divine protection, therefore false. To surrender to a foreign nation was ignominy. They would have no part of it, nor would they tolerate the one who preached it. But Jeremiah received his message from God, and could only deliver it as it was received.

1) *The Message* (27:1-22)

(a) *Nations must serve Babylon* (27:1-11). Ambassadors from each of the neighboring kings of Edom, Moab, Ammon, Tyre, and Sidon had come to Zedekiah, very likely with the thought of discussing the possibilities of a coalition against the rising Babylonian power (27:3). Just as God had used Jeremiah to speak to His people Judah, so Jeremiah was given a message to deliver to these foreign nations. He was not only given the words to speak but he was instructed how to demonstrate them symbolically. He was to make a yoke[19] (wooden bars connected by cords) and put it upon his neck, symbolizing bondage to Babylon (27:2-

---

[18]A comparison of associated references points to a textual corruption in the name "Jehoiakim" of 27:1. As the margin of the American Standard Version states, this should be rendered "Zedekiah" (cf. 27:3,12,20; 28:1). Both chapters 27 and 28 deal with events of the same year. It is to be noted also that 27:1 is omitted from the Septuagint Version. See Schaff, *op. cit.*, pp. 243-44, for a discussion of this textual question.

[19]Whether Jeremiah was to make one yoke or five cannot be determined from the text. More likely he sent a yoke with each ambassador. At least one yoke never reached its destination, because of the rash action of a false prophet (28:10).

4; cf. 28:13). The interpretation involved the following message from God:

The fact of sovereignty: "I have made the earth, the men and the beasts . . . and I give it [the land of the nations] unto whom it seemeth right unto me" (27:5).

The exercise of sovereignty: "And now have I given all these lands into the hand of Nebuchadnezzar the king of Babylon, my servant. . . . And all the nations shall serve him . . . until the time of his own land come" (27:6-7).

The warning of sovereignty: To refuse to submit to Babylon's yoke was to bring punishment (27:8). To hearken to false prophets, diviners or soothsayers was to believe a lie (27:9-10). To submit to Babylon's yoke assured at least peaceful dwelling in the land (27:11).

(b) *Judah must serve Babylon* (27:12-15). Not only were the foreign nations to be brought under Nebuchadnezzar's yoke but Judah also would have to submit. Two options existed for the nation. She could resist the conqueror to the bitter end and thereby be virtually wiped out "by the sword, by the famine, and by the pestilence" (27:13), or she could serve Nebuchadnezzar in his land and live. Jeremiah pleaded for the latter choice.

(c) *The temple vessels must be given to Babylon* (27:16-22). Here again Jeremiah met his opponents, the false prophets, head on. They had been prophesying that the temple vessels which Nebuchadnezzar had taken in the first deportation (27:20; II Kings 24:1-17) would shortly be returned to Judah (27:16). "It is a lie!" exclaimed Jeremiah (27:16). He challenged that the people might test the authority of the false prophets by having them intercede to God in behalf of the temple vessels remaining—the costly bronze bases (I Kings 7:27-36), pillars (I Kings 7:15), wash basin ("sea," I Kings 7:23-26), and other precious vessels —that they be not taken to Babylon as well (27:18). Time would bring the test of that authority for, insisted Jeremiah, those vessels "shall be carried to Babylon," to remain there until it was God's time to return them. "Until the day that I visit them, saith Jehovah; then will I bring them up, and restore them to this place" (27:22).

2) *Opposition to the Message Judged* (28:1-17). The people might have waited until the destruction of the holy city to be convinced whether Jeremiah or his opponents gave the false prophecy—by the test caustically suggested by Jeremiah (27:18). But they were given immediate demonstration for such a test. God singled out one false prophet, Hananiah of Gibeon, and publicly judged him by death for his false preaching.

Hananiah was a prophet of false peace. He recognized the power of Babylon, for Nebuchadnezzar had proved that power by taking Jeconiah captive with many people and the temple vessels in the recent deportation. But Hananiah publicly prophesied the lie that within two full years Babylon's power would be crushed and the captives of Judah returned (28:2-4,11). Jeremiah openly challenged him, acknowledging the attractiveness of his optimistic outlook (28:6) but reminding him that the true prophets of God who preceded them both had prophesied of war and pestilence, not peace (28:7-9). Hananiah countered

Jeremiah's fearless challenge by boldly snatching the yoke's wooden bar (chap. 27) from Jeremiah's neck and breaking it, saying that God had said, "Even so will I break the yoke of Nebuchadnezzar" (28:11).

Now God, desiring to give the immediate test to the false prophet who had misrepresented His Word, sent His true prophet to Hananiah with two messages: the broken bars of wood would be replaced by unbreakable bars of iron (28:13), and Hananiah would die before the year was out, for speaking rebellion against God (28:16).

The message of this chapter is very pertinent to the present world system. There is much talk of peace. The human heart would want to see peace (cf. "Amen: Jehovah do so," 28:6). But the prophecies of God's Word— true prophecies—speak not of peace but of wars for the end times. A nation may *appear* to thwart the just and righteous plan of God by breaking the wooden bars of a yoke, but the iron bars of His irresistible power reveal themselves in every instance.

"So Hananiah the [false] prophet died the same year" (28:17).

And just a few years later, all "peace sermons" to the contrary notwithstanding, the holy city of the prophets' controversy was destroyed.

3) *Other False Prophets Judged* (29:1-32). Consisting of letters written at different times, this chapter expands on subjects already recorded in this section of the book of Jeremiah, namely, Jeremiah's message, the opposition of the false prophets, and their judgment.

The first letter recorded is that which Jeremiah sent "unto the residue of the elders of the captivity" of the first deportation, probably written a year or two after they reached Babylon, in the first years of Zedekiah's reign (29:1-3). The letter discusses three subjects:

(a) The captives in Babylon were to settle down and live as normally as possible under the circumstances (build houses, marry, multiply, seek the peace of the land, and pray for the land, 29:5-7). Seventy years later, a new generation was to be led back to the land of Judah and restored to the former relationship with Jehovah (29:10-14).

(b) The king and the people of Judah which had not been taken captive in the first deportation were to suffer by the sword, famine, and pestilence for not hearkening to the words of Jehovah (29:15-20).

(c) Two false prophets, Ahab and Zedekiah,[20] were to be delivered over to the hand of Nebuchadnezzar and be slain before the people's eyes, as an example for other prophets living in sin and falsely representing God's words (29:21-23). This third part of Jeremiah's letter to the residue in captivity introduces the subject of the remainder of chapter 29, the false prophets.

The second reference to letters in the chapter is to a letter (or letters)[21] sent by the false prophet Shemaiah to the priest Zephaniah, intended to be read by all the people and the priests. The letter itself, quoted verbatim here (29:26-28), reprimanded Zephaniah for not performing his duties regarding radical prophets in not arresting "Jeremiah of Anathoth, who maketh himself a prophet unto you" (29:26-28). Grammatically, the opening phrase of

[20]No more is known of these than the identifications given here.
[21]The Hebrew text allows for either "letter" or "letters." If there was just one letter, it was circulated for reading by all the priests and the people.

29:25, "because thou hast sent letters," is left dangling without the anticipated "therefore" after verse 28. Jeremiah wished to supply the essence of the "therefore" in recording the circumstances of the third letter of the chapter (29:30-32). He was commanded by God to send this third letter to the people of the captivity to report the sin of Shemaiah, that of having caused the people to "trust in a lie," and his judgment (note the previously expected "therefore"), which was to be deprivation of male offspring to perpetuate his name, and death without seeing good come to God's people.

* * *

Thus Jeremiah's unpopular message withstood his opponents' destructive plots because it was *God's* message. And God's message, being truth, must inevitably slay falsehood.

B. The Ultimate Deliverance (30:1—33:26)

The four chapters of this section present one theme: the consolatory hope of salvation in ultimate deliverance from physical and spiritual bondage. Chapters 32 and 33 are dated during the siege of Jerusalem, in the tenth year of Zedekiah's reign, while Jeremiah was imprisoned in the court of the guard (32:1-2; 33:1). Chapters 30 and 31, though not dated, were probably written either during the siege or immediately after the fall of the city.

So it was during the darkest hour of the experience of God's people that their prophet, himself a prisoner, was given to see and record prophetic visions of future glory and blessing beyond brightest human dreams. The theme of the righteous judgments of God had filled the record of the book of Jeremiah up to this point. Now, on the eve of the calamitous event of judgment, the grace of God was in prominent view as another ingredient of the divine solution, precipitated by the catalyst of the heart of God's people turning to repentance in a future day. Countless men and women of all the ages, in their darkest hour of desperate need, have experienced the light of God's grace and mercy as they thrust themselves unreservedly, in faith, into the hands of God.

1. *A Returned People* (30:1—31:26)

At this point in the book of Jeremiah, over half has been the recording of the prophet's message of "pluck up and . . . break down" (1:10). It is not surprising, therefore, that such an intense, though relatively unlengthy, concentration of the bright message of "build and . . . plant" (1:10) should appear. God told Jeremiah explicitly to record the total message in a book: "Write thee all the words that I have spoken unto thee in a book" (30:2). The words recorded thereafter are the words of the "return to the land" (30:3). The time of the fulfillment of the prophecy is indicated by the words "lo, the days come" (30:3). It appears that this phrase has *end times* primarily in view, not the days of a return from the Babylonian exile, for these reasons:

1) Similar phrases throughout the book of Jeremiah refer to end times (cf. 3:16; 16:14; 23:5).

2) There is explicit reference in this section (chaps. 30—33) to end or latter times: "in the latter days ye shall understand it. At that time . . ." (30:24b—31:1a).

3) This section of Jeremiah in the large scope is predominantly a prophecy of the far future (e.g., the new covenant, 31:31).

4) If the judgment of Jeremiah's prophecy had the

catastrophic proportions of uprooting and destroying the nation, the prophecy of a mere temporary and partial restoration would be anticlimactic. The design of God is eventual restoration of His glory in the midst of His people at the end of time, and upon this the prophecies of chapters 30 through 33 focus primary attention, however relevant were the words to the events of a near future.

The section 30:1—31:26 may be outlined according to the people that the words of the prophecy concern. First, both houses of Israel and Judah are spoken of (30:4-22). Then, only Israel, or Ephraim, is the subject (30:23—31:22). Finally, Judah's share of the salvation is described (31:23-26).

a. Israel and Judah (30:4-22). These are words "concerning Israel and concerning Judah" (30:4). Jehovah views the pain and paleness of His people, and describes the condition as "the time of Jacob's trouble" (30:5-7). This is a reference to the Day of the Lord in the end times, when there will be intense tribulation and persecution for the Jewish people under the dominion of Gentile nations among whom they have been scattered (30:8,11). But that tribulation shall not be forever, for Jacob "shall be saved out of it" (30:7) by Jehovah who is with him, though such a deliverance is not without corrective judgment (30:11). The picture is repeated again in the paragraph 30:12-17. The hurt of Jehovah's people is seemingly incurable, their wound grievous (30:12). The cause was the increase of their sins (30:15). But Jehovah promised, "I will restore health unto thee, and I will heal thee of thy wounds" (30:17).

In the restoration, when the dwelling places and cities and palace will be rebuilt, then thanksgiving, joy, increase of families, glory, and stability will return to God's people, "as aforetime. . . . And," said Jehovah, "Ye shall be my people, and I will be your God" (30:18-22). This description of restoration of glory could only have reference to the future millennial kingdom of God's chosen people.

b. Israel (30:23—31:22). This section treats in great detail the future restoration of Israel (or Ephraim[22]). The discussion of Judah's restoration is offered in a much shorter paragraph (31:23-26). This may be because, as one commentator has put it, "the ten tribes, who had long languished in exile, had the least hope, according to man's estimation, of deliverance."[23] The longer prophecy emphasizes the fact of the sureness of Ephraim's share in the Messianic salvation. This may also explain why God called Ephraim His firstborn (31:9).[24]

The words of paragraph 30:23-24, which appeared earlier at 23:19-20, are used to introduce the subject of this section about Ephraim. Judgments of Jehovah's "sweeping tempest" and "fierce anger" which would "burst upon the head of the wicked," to be felt even in the "latter days" (30:24) are cited. Then 31:1 commences with the phrase "at that time"—in other words, in the latter days. At this point, the prophecies of ultimate restoration for Israel are described.

The tone of these prophecies about Ephraim's return which is one of endearing fatherly love reveals the main intent of the prophecies. The following examples bear this out: "At that time. . . will I be the God of all the

---

[22]Ephraim, the favored grandson of Rachel whom Jacob treated as his firstborn, is considered in this and other parts of Scripture as the head and representative of the ten northern tribes of Israel. Hence "Ephraim" may be equated with the term "Israel."

[23]Keil and Delitzsch, *op. cit.,* II, 21.

[24]*Ibid.,* p. 22.

families of Israel, and they shall be my people" (31:1); "Yea, I have loved thee with an everlasting love . . ." (31:3); "for I am a father to Israel, and Ephraim is my first-born" (31:9); "Is Ephraim my dear son? Is he a darling child? . . . my heart yearneth for him; I will surely have mercy on him" (31:20).

The last sentence of the section is an appropriate conclusion to the message of Israel's return. It prophesies a "new thing," a new situation: "A woman shall encompass a man" (31:22). The Hebrew word for *encompass* may be translated "embrace," so that the intention of the picture is that whereas the man (Jehovah) has embraced the woman (Israel) in love, the latter days would see a different situation: Israel (the woman) will seek after, embrace, and cling to her lover, God (the man; cf. Hosea 2:19).

c. Judah (31:23-26). Few words are spoken here concerning Judah's share of millennial blessing, but the paucity of words magnifies the glory of the fact that when the cities of Judah are, as it were, rebuilt, and the city dwellers and farmers (husbandmen) live together as one nation, then the happy and glorious words of the benediction will resound again across the land, "Jehovah bless thee, O habitation of righteousness, O mountain of holiness" (31:23). The benediction will be genuine and non-hypocritical, a *song of blessing,* because the weary and sorrowful soul will have been satiated by the Lord of glory (31:25).

2. A Complete Renovation (31:27-40)

A new section begins with 31:27 as seen by the following: (1) verse 26 comprises a natural concluding statement to all that went before, being the happy testimony of the prophet for having had such a "sweet" sleep, or state of ecstasy, in which God revealed to him the consolatory promises; (2) the phrase "Behold, the days come," appearing at the beginning of three of the four paragraphs, reveals the unity of this section; and (3) the central subject of the section is the future innovation of the *new,* especially the new covenant.

a. *A New Outlook* (31:27-30). First, there would be a new beginning of the people of God, sown by God "with the seed of man, and with the seed of beast" (31:27). Second, there would be a new relationship with God. For in the past, before the captivity, He had watched over the people "to pluck up and to break down," but now it would be "to build and to plant" (31:28). Third, there would be a new emphasis of the accountability of each individual to God. Although God had always legislated individual accountability for sin in the past, corporate life, or family-unit living, was the general pattern into which the Israelites had woven their lives, giving rise to the proverb "The *fathers* have eaten sour grapes, and the *children's* teeth are set on edge" (31:29). In the new day, it would be made more clear that God was essentially dealing with individual hearts, so that "every one shall die for his own iniquity" (31:30).

b. *A New Covenant* (31:31-37). The New Testament sheds the most light on this passage. Much of the passage is quoted in Hebrews 8:8-13, and 10:15-17; the phrase "new covenant" appears in Luke 22:20. From the context of the quotations it is obvious that the new or second covenant replaced the old or first covenant because the old covenant did not, could not, nor was it intended to, save. Associated with the old covenant were outward ordinances and objects (Heb. 9:1-10) which were not intended to save but rather to teach the sinfulness of sin and the lost condition of men, and point to (prefigure, typify) Christ as Saviour. Jeremiah records that the people of Israel broke God's old covenant by teaching the law to others but not living by it themselves (31:32). Under the new covenant, the law would not be annulled but would be written "in their inward parts, and in their heart" (31:33). They would *know God personally,* for which there would be soul salvation by forgiveness of sin (31: 34). While God in Jeremiah's prophecy does not identify sacrifice or blood with this new covenant, this way of forgiveness is taught by the author of Hebrews. The inviolability and indestructiveness of the ordinances of God, and therefore of His new covenant, are emphatically stated at this point in 31:35-37.

c. A New City (31:38-40). This prophecy points out again the dual intent of the prophetic element. The city of Mt. Zion would be rebuilt and enlarged, and even its valley of dead bodies and ashes would be "holy unto Jehovah." This is the miracle of divine renovation and sanctification. Further, holy Jerusalem would remain forever, even beyond the last days. This must be a reference to the new Jerusalem of Revelation 21:2, the holy city that shall never pass away.

3. The Test of Faith (32:1—33:26)

In the tenth year of Zedekiah, while Babylon's army was besieging Jerusalem, Jeremiah was imprisoned in the court of the guard for prophesying the fall of the city (32:1-5; cf. also 37:21; 38:13, 28). It was at this time that his faith in God's word of restoration (chaps. 30-31) was put to a live test. Even while the city was in siege,

Jeremiah was told through his cousin Hanamel to buy a plot of ground in Anathoth. God had foretold the details of this contact with Hanamel, and Jeremiah knew when the contact was made that it was God's will for him to buy the field (32:8), even though, from a human standpoint, it was a foolhardy transaction. According to God's instructions, Jeremiah told Baruch, his secretary, to deposit the deeds in an earthen jar, for God had said that "houses and fields and vineyards shall yet again be bought in this land" (32:11-15).

After obeying God's instructions (32:6-15), Jeremiah reflected on the logic of the purchase, and his faith wavered. The core of his objection is seen immediately when one reads 32:24-25 in connection with 32:17a[25] thus:

> Ah Lord Jehovah! behold (v. 17) Behold, the mounds,[26] they are come unto the city to take it (v. 24); And thou hast said . . . Buy thee the field for money, and call witnesses (v. 25a).

"But," the confused prophet exclaimed, "the city is given into the hand of the Chaldeans!" (32:25).

The answer of God to the doubt of the prophet has been the classic answer to doubters of all the ages since:

> Behold, I am Jehovah, the God of all flesh:
> IS THERE ANYTHING TOO HARD FOR ME? (32:27).

God then proceeded to rehearse the sequence of His will for His people and the land: (1) the judgment (32:28-29), (2) the causes for the judgment (32:30-35), and (3) the restoration (32:37-44). The logical basis for buying fields in the land of present battle was stated by Jehovah thus: "Like as I have brought all this great

[25]The record in the intervening verses is a descriptive acknowledgment of the power and sovereignty of God.

[26]The mounds were high embankments located outside the walls of the city, from which assault was made on the city.

evil upon this people, so will I bring upon them all the the good that I have promised them" (32:42).

A second message from God came to Jeremiah while he was still a prisoner of Zedekiah, reassuring the prophet of His mighty hand to accomplish by deed the words of His consolatory promises: "Call unto me, and I will answer thee, and will show thee great things, and difficult,[27] which thou knowest not" (33:3). But how would God accomplish such things? The clue is given in the paragraph 33:14-18, which is the key to the chapter. God reasserts that He would "perform that good word which I have spoken concerning the house of Israel and concerning the house of Judah" (33:14). The method of the performance is in the raising up of a "Branch of righteousness" of the line of David, that is, a king who would reign in righteousness.

A similar message had been given some years earlier, during Zedekiah's reign, quoted in 23:5-8. There the king was to be identified by the name *Jehovah Tsidkenu,* or "Jehovah our righteousness." Now, at the hour of the siege of the city, Jehovah says the city ("she") would be called "Jehovah our righteousness" (33:16). The common key word is *righteousness.* The righteous rule will bring a righteous city, because a righteous king is to be concerned with maintaining constant fellowship between the people and God (hence *continual* sacrifices and offerings, 33:18). And if there is such a fellowship, then there is the favor of God, described thus: "Behold, I will bring it [the city] health and cure. . . abundance of peace and truth" (33:6). "And this city shall be to me for a name

---

[27]The Hebrew word here translated "difficult" is literally "fortified," therefore probably meaning "inaccessible, unattainable," that is, unable to be altered or even touched by man.

of joy, for a praise and for a glory" (33:9). As surely as the covenant of day and night remains unbreakable, so these blessed promises of the spiritual covenant cannot be broken (33:19-26).

Jerusalem has never yet seen a full measure of such restoration and renovation. The restoration period of the return from captivity was a partial and temporary thing. The ultimate fulfillment of the promise is to come one day when the Messiah, who supremely fulfills the name "Jehovah our righteousness," rules over His people in the glorious reign of righteousness.

II. DAYS OF FULFILLMENT (34:1—44:30)

THE BOOK OF JEREMIAH is unique among the prophetic books in that the very fulfillment of the events of its main prophecy, the fall of Jerusalem and the captivity under Babylon, is recorded as a substantial part of the account.[28] Chapters 34 through 44 comprise this segment, recording the siege of Jerusalem (chaps. 34-38), its fall (chap. 39), and events after the fall (chaps. 40-44).

A. The Siege of Jerusalem (34:1—38:28)

These chapters do not follow a chronological sequence.[29] Rather, they were placed in their present order to present a topical theme centered around the prophet and his message, as seen in the following outline:

1. *Outcome of Siege Restated* (34:1-7)

While Nebuchadnezzar's army was fighting against Jerusalem and its surrounding cities, including Judah's

---

[28]Of course the prophecies were spoken and written *before* the fulfillment.

[29]For the chapters identified with Zedekiah's reign, Howard Kuist suggests this probable chronological order: 34:1-7; 37:1-10; 34:8-22; 37:11-21; 38:1-28. Kuist, *op. cit.*, p. 332.

THEME:	REFERENCE:				CONTENT:			KINGS OF JUDAH:
The outcome of siege restated	34:1				KING AND THE PEOPLE	Captivity		Z E D E K I A H
The sin of the people renewed	34:8					Disobedience		Z E D E K I A H
	35:1							JEHOIAKIM
The prophet of God apprehended	36:1				KING AND THE PROPHET	Princes for, king against Jeremiah		JEHOIAKIM
		37:1				King for, princes against Jeremiah		Z E D E K I A H
			37:21					

94

two remaining fortified cities, Lachish and Azekah[30] (34:1, 6-7), God sent Jeremiah to Zedekiah to again foretell the outcome of the siege: "Behold, I will give this city into the hand of the king of Babylon" (34:2). Zedekiah's personal lot was also revealed: he was to be taken captive to Babylon (34:4), though he would not die by the sword (34:5).

2. *Sin of the People Renewed* (34:8—35:19)

No background information is given in connection with the events of this section. We may presume, however, that while the siege of Jerusalem was going on, Zedekiah and the people were thinking of all ways to repel the Chaldean army. Hoping no doubt to procure the favor of Jehovah by obeying one of His commandments originating in the early life of the Israelites, Zedekiah covenanted with the people, before God, to revive the law of proclaiming liberty to Hebrew servants after six years' service.[31] Zedekiah no doubt had also hoped by this action to inspire the freed servants to a more intense defense of the city. Not long after the liberation, the Chaldeans suspended their siege temporarily, when they saw Pharaoh's army coming to help Judah (37:1-10). On seeing the Chaldeans retreat, Zedekiah and the people reneged on the liberation covenant they had made, and brought the freed slaves back into servitude, thereby incurring the guilt of profaning God's name, since He had been witness to the covenant (34:11, 16). Their sin was that of disobedience: "You have not obeyed Me in pro-

[30]Lachish was about 23 miles southwest of Jerusalem; Azekah was located about 18 miles west-southwest of Jerusalem (cf. Joshua 10:11; I Sam. 17:1; Neh. 11:30). Both cities, located on roads to Jerusalem, were important for the holy city's defense.

[31]See Exodus 21:1 ff.; Leviticus 25:39-41. Actually, it appears that Zedekiah freed virtually *all* servants at this time.

claiming liberty . . ." (34:17, Berkeley Version). The consequences for breaking the covenant are described in 34:17-22. The king, the leaders and the people were to be given into the hand of their enemies, and the cities were to be made a desolation without inhabitant.

The account of chapter 35[32] serves to expose the glaring sin of disobedience described in the previous chapter by relating the story of the obedience of a group of migrant families called the Rechabites. These tent dwellers (35:10) were a branch of the Kenites who located generally in the southern regions of Judah.[33] They were loyal to the code of living prescribed by the founders of their puritanic order, Rechab and his son Jonadab. The code was intended to preserve them in their nomadic culture, keeping them from what were considered to be the degenerating influences of wine, settled town life, and farming (35:8-9). The Rechabites had come to Jerusalem at this time (c. 605 B.C.) for refuge from the armies of Chaldea and Aram (35:11). When at the direction of Jehovah, Jeremiah offered them some wine,[34] the beverage of the vineyard, they refused it on the basis of their obedience to their fathers: "We have. . . obeyed, and done according to all that Jonadab our father commanded us" (35:10).[35] This was the example that Jehovah wanted to show His

[32]The events of chapter 35 took place during Jehoiakim's reign (35:1). The chapter is placed here apparently because of its illustration of obedience, the antithesis of the disobedience exemplified in chapter 34.

[33]See Judges 1:16; I Samuel 15:6; 27:10; I Chronicles 2:55.

[34]God, knowing what the outcome of this test would be, planned to use it as an example for the Israelites.

[35]They were forced, by the Chaldean invasion, to forsake their tents for the houses of the walled city. Therefore they did not violate the spirit of the Rechabite code. Such is the intent of the words of 35:11.

own people. Said He, "They [the Rechabites] obey their father's commandment: but I have spoken unto you, rising up early and speaking; and ye have not hearkened unto me" (35:14). Judah was reaping judgment for her disobedience (35:17), while the Rechabites were promised an eternal relationship to God for their obedience (35:19).

3. *The Prophet of God Apprehended* (36:1—38:28)

Jeremiah's experiences with two kings and their princes are described in these three chapters. Actually, chapter 36 is not a chapter of the siege of Jerusalem, since its action is dated in the fourth year of King Jehoiakim (36:1). It may have been placed here because of its contribution to the story of Jeremiah's personal relations with the kings and princes toward the end of his prophetic ministry.

a. The Princes Protect Jeremiah; the King Opposes Him (36:1-32). This is the story of the first actual recording of the prophecy of Jeremiah. God commanded the prophecy to be written on the usual roll[36] (36:1-4). The message was to concern Israel, Judah, and the foreign nations. Baruch, Jeremiah's secretary, wrote what Jeremiah dictated to him. Next, the prophecy was to be read to all the people which were gathered in the temple on a fast day (36:5-10). Such a day arrived in the ninth month of the fifth year of Jehoiakim.[37] One who heard Baruch's reading was Micaiah, who then reported to the princes the

---

[36]Sheets of papyrus were fastened together, the entire length being then rolled up for handling. The codex, or book form, did not appear until near the end of the Apostolic Age or later.

[37]It is not known what the occasion for the fast day was. It may have been a memorial to a previous national tragedy. At any rate, it was Jeremiah's hope that the message of the prophecy would reach hearts which, in the spirit of fasting, were in an attitude of soul-searching.

essence of the prophecy (36:11-19). The princes in turn sent for Baruch, who read all the words of the prophecy to them. Struck with fear and apprehension over the message, they informed Baruch that they would have to report such an ominous message to the king, but urged Baruch and Jeremiah to go into secret hiding for their lives. This was the princes' protection of the prophet.

When the contents of the prophecy were reported to King Jehoiakim, his reaction was violently negative (36: 20-26). After Jehudi read a few columns of the roll, the king gave vent to his wrath by cutting up the roll and burning it in the fire before him, despite the urgings of three princes not to do so. Moreover, Jehoiakim commanded that Jeremiah and Baruch be apprehended, "but Jehovah hid them" (36:26).

God not only protected the prophet but He also preserved the prophecy by having it rewritten on another roll (36:27-32). It was to contain "all the former words that were in the first roll" (36:28), plus "many like words," the additional section possibly being as large as the original section.[38]

b. The Princes Oppose Jeremiah; the King Protects Him (37:1—38:28). The experiences of Jeremiah with King Zedekiah and the princes under him are related, with the focus of attention returning to the time of the final siege of Jerusalem. Zedekiah was disobedient to God, as were also the people, but he nevertheless kept Jeremiah available to him, for in his vacillating spirit there seemed to be hope that God would not let His holy city fall. When Pharaoh's army came to help Judah against the Babylon-

---

[38]The Hebrew word for "like" (36:32) may intend to give the meaning "as many as they." See Appendix I.

ians, Zedekiah sought Jeremiah's intercession to God: "Pray now unto Jehovah our God for us" (37:3). But God directed Jeremiah to tell Zedekiah that Pharaoh's army would soon be returning to Egypt, and that the Chaldeans would renew the siege to its ultimate completion (37:6-10).

While the Chaldeans' siege was still in suspension, Jeremiah was seen by Irijah, captain of the ward, going out of the city to the north, apparently heading for Anathoth. Charged with desertion—"falling away to the Chaldeans"—the prophet was brought to the princes, "who smote him and put him in prison." After many days Zedekiah brought him to his house, where he asked him secretly, "Is there any word from Jehovah?" (37:17). Jeremiah's reply confirmed the previous prophecies, that captivity to Babylon was inevitable. In the same reply Jeremiah, innocent of the princes' charge of desertion, pleaded with Zedekiah not to send him back to prison. The king granted his plea by transferring him to the more livable quarters of the court of the guard (37:17-21). That he did not give him complete freedom is explained by the fact that the king feared vetoing the action of his princes.

But Jeremiah's stay in the court of the guard was shortlived. Some of the princes, who had heard Jeremiah speak the prophecy of doom, besought Zedekiah to put the prophet to death for weakening the morale of the fighting forces (38:1-4). Weak Zedekiah submitted to their demands and committed Jeremiah into their merciless hands, saying, "The king is not he that can do anything against you" (38:5). At this the princes cast the prophet into a deep, waterless cistern, letting him down by cords to the bottom of the pit, where he sank into the mire, and was left to die.

This was the moment of truth for Jeremiah. For forty years he had faithfully served God by preaching a true though unpopular message, and though he had experienced the hand of God with him many times before, this was the ultimate test. The people were not with him. Friends were wanting. The king had no moral or ethical backbone, not to speak of his spiritual infidelity. The princes, so unlike those under King Jehoiakim, had left him for dead. One alone remained to help him—God. If His Word were true, Jeremiah had to live to see the day of Jerusalem's fall. God, as is His way so often, used an insignificant person to touch off Jeremiah's rescue. The man was a servant in the king's house, an Ethiopian eunuch, Ebed-melech by name. He persuaded Zedekiah not to let the prophet die in the pit; at the king's command, with the help of other men,[39] he drew the prophet up out of the pit (38:7-13).

After Jeremiah was rescued, King Zedekiah sent for him to inquire again if there were any new word from God (38:14-23). "Hide nothing from me," commanded the king, still hoping for a change in the message of the prophet. Jeremiah reiterated his usual message. Zedekiah then admitted his fear of the Jews who had already fallen captive to the Chaldeans, lest they deliver him over to the enemy. Jeremiah guaranteed him the safety of his life on one condition: "Obey. . . the voice of Jehovah, in that

---

[39]The text says "thirty men." The Hebrew construction giving the number is unusual. The Septuagint reads "three men," which may have been the correct number. See Charles F. Pfeiffer and Everett F. Harrison (eds.), *The Wycliffe Bible Commentary* (Chicago: Moody Press, 1962), p. 683.

which I speak unto thee: so it shall be well with thee, and thy soul shall live" (38:20). Zedekiah commanded the prophet not to divulge the details of this conversation to the princes, a confidence that Jeremiah kept (38:24-27).

And so God, overruling the fatal plots of the princes and the impotent throne of Zedekiah, preserved His prophet from death during the months of siege. And "Jeremiah abode in the court of the guard until the day that Jerusalem was taken" (38:28). Chapter 39 records the events of that fall.

B. The Fall of Jerusalem (39:1-18)

After eighteen long months of bitter siege, when the food supply of the city had been depleted, the first breach was made in the city's walls, and Jerusalem fell to its enemy. The date was 586 B.C., in the eleventh year of Zedekiah's reign (39:1-2).

This chapter serves as a fitting climax to all that has gone before, as fulfillment answers to prophecy.[40] The long forty years of Jeremiah's prophetic preaching were on trial during the painfully slow months of the siege. Was his message true, or was he just another false prophet? Would Jerusalem fall, or would Nebuchadrezzar be driven back to Babylon in shame and humility? The breach in the walls of the city was the first abrupt sound in the thunderous reply. *The prophet had spoken the truth.*

1. *The Toll* (39:4-10)

When Zedekiah and his armies saw the Babylonian

---

[40]The book of Jeremiah does not conclude at this point, however. There are sequels to the event as far as the land of Judah is concerned (chaps. 40-45). And there are prophecies against the foreign nations (chaps. 46-51). Chapter 52, a restatement of the fall of Jerusalem, then serves as the appropriate conclusion to the book. (The fall of Jerusalem is described in two other Bible portions: II Kings 24:18—25:30; II Chronicles 36:17-21.)

princes[41] sitting in counsel at the middle gate apparently plotting their next moves, the king and his men fled toward the Jordan Valley, or the depression of Arabah, but were overtaken in the plains of Jericho and delivered to Nebuchadrezzar at Riblah, the northern boundary city of Palestine.[42] There Zedekiah's sons and all the nobles of Judah were slain before his eyes. As for Zedekiah, his eyes were torturously put out, and in agony and shame he was carried to Babylon in chains, living the rest of his life in prison (39:6-7; 52:11). The toll list of the fallen city is recorded briefly in 39:8-10:

1) All houses were burned; the walls were broken down.
2) Most of the inhabitants were taken captive to Babylon.
3) The poorest of the people were allowed to remain in the land, to keep the vineyards and fields.

2. *Two Men Delivered* (39:11-18)

a. Jeremiah's deliverance is given in sparse detail. When the paragraph 39:11-14 is harmonized with 40:1, the following sequence may be constructed: At the express command of Nebuchadrezzar, Nebuzaradan, captain of the guard, had Jeremiah released from the court of the guard, and committed him to Gedaliah, who was appointed to be governor of the cities of Judah. While the vast undertaking of transferring all the captives to Babylon was going on, Jeremiah had the liberty of mixing with the people ("so he dwelt among the people," 39:14b), no doubt comforting them and instructing them how they

---

[41]Three of the princes' names are mentioned (not six men, as 39:3 was formerly thought to convey): Nergal-sharezer, whose office was Shamgar-nebo; Sarsechim, whose office was Rab-saris, or chief of the eunuchs; and Nergal-sharezer, whose office was Rab-mag.

[42]Riblah was a junction city connecting Palestine with Babylon.

should live as captives in a strange land. In what must have been utter confusion during those days of mass deportation, Jeremiah was not recognized by the soldiers and, like the others of the crowd, he was placed in chains and put in the "train" of captives. At Ramah he was identified by the officials and released by Nebuzaradan (40: 1), his real freedom beginning at that moment.

b. Ebed-melech's deliverance is only implied in the paragraph 39:15-18. The paragraph itself very likely fits chronologically after 38:13, recounting God's reward to Ebed-melech for his part in Jeremiah's deliverance from the dungeon (38:7-13). Since the story of chapter 38 centers about Jeremiah, the insert of the paragraph about Ebed-melech in the middle of chapter 38 would have broken the continuity of the account. The promise of deliverance to the Ethiopian eunuch in the day of Jerusalem's fall is very appropriately located here at the end of chapter 39, after the deliverance of Jeremiah is described. A precious truth is taught here, namely, that God does not forget *any* of His children—for even as He delivered His prophet, so He also delivered the lowly servant.

C. Events in Judah After Jerusalem's Fall (40:1—44:30)

The last years of Jeremiah's life were spent mainly in mournful retrospect, though this aspect of his experiences is not recorded in his prophecy. The retrospect was toward one sight: the heap of ruins of the beloved city. The prophet must have shed many tears over its destruction, and more tears over the scattering of its people. Jeremiah very likely wrote the five mournful chapters of Lamentations very soon after the city fell.[43] The very first word of Lamentations is *'eka,* meaning "alas!"

That which is recorded in the book of Jeremiah concerning the prophet's last years is basically twofold: the series of events leading up to his deportation to Egypt, and the last of his prophecies in his prophetic office. The details of his death are lacking, and we learn only from tradition that his death was by stoning and that he was buried in Egypt.

So in the sense in which the book of Jeremiah tells the story of the man of Anathoth in his prophetic office, the climax is reached in chapter 39. The atmosphere seems at this point to change from increasing intensity to one of sad but not sulking acceptance of the judgments of God. Whereas the spotlight of attention had been aimed at Judah and Jerusalem, now it focuses on Nebuchadrezzar and the foreign nations, and only incidentally on the Jews left in Judah as they react to Nebuchadrezzar's throne.

1. *Governorship of Gedaliah* (40:1—41:18)

a. *Jeremiah's Liberty Assured* (40:1-6). Nebuchadrezzar appointed Gedaliah, son of Ahikam, to govern the scattered poor people left in Judah to keep the fields and vineyards (40:5). Nebuzaradan gave Jeremiah the choice to either live in Babylon under favorable living conditions ("I will look well unto thee," 40:4), or to remain in Judah ("whither it seemeth good and right unto thee to go, thither go," 40:4). Jeremiah, true to the place of his heart, chose Judah for his home, dwelling at Mizpah "among the people that were left in the land" (40:6).[44]

---

[43]See the excellent introduction to Lamentations in Pfeiffer and Harrison, *op. cit.,* pp. 695-96.

[44]Mizpah, located near Ramah, a few miles north of Jerusalem, had apparently escaped much of the devastating plunder of the Chaldean armies.

b. Nebuchadrezzar's Governor Assassinated (40:13—
41:18). On taking office, Governor Gedaliah made it
known to the Jews what kind of citizens he expected them
to be. They were to be obedient to the rule of the Chaldeans, and were to faithfully till the soil. In return they
could expect normal peaceful living conditions (40:9).
Gedaliah would be their representative before the Chaldeans (40:10). The governor announced this policy of
state to the Jewish military units (40:7-8) and to other
Jews returning from their flight to surrounding nations
(40:11-12). They assented to the rule and so applied
themselves to the tasks of gathering the late summer
fruits and olives, and of making wine, to keep them sup-
plied through the forthcoming winter season.[45]

But not all the Jews left in the land were reconciled to
subjection to Babylon's throne. And so it was that Ishmael, son of Nethaniah and a relative of Zedekiah, spon-
sored by Baalis, king of the Ammonites, came to Mizpah
with ten other men and in the course of what was sup-
posed to be a friendly meal rose up and slew Gedaliah,
his officers, and all the Jews that were with him (40:13—
41:3).

On the second day after the secret assassination of the
governor, eighty men, in a state of mourning (apparently
over Jerusalem's fall) were on their way to Jerusalem to
present meal offerings and frankincense at the "house of
Jehovah," that is, at the site of the ruined temple. Either
the fact of their being a sizable band of men frightened
Ishmael, or the fact of their religious mourning pricked
his conscience. The text does not reveal the motive, but
Ishmael and his men slew seventy of the band, ten being

---

[45]Jerusalem was destroyed in the middle of the summer season.

spared for their bribe of wheat, barley, oil, and honey (41:4-9). The slaying of the seventy precipitated a larger engagement by Ishmael, at the end of which all the people round about Mizpah were taken captive (41:9-10). When news of this reached Johanan, son of Kareath, he rallied some forces and went to fight with Ishmael, at the waters of Gibeon. In the encounter Ishmael's captives fled over to Johanan's side, while Ishmael and eight of his men were able to escape to Ammon (41:11-15).

The outcome of the assassination of Gedaliah was crucial in that it eventually spelled death for the Jews who had just begun a peaceful existence in the land. Out of fear of reprisal by Nebuchadrezzar for Gedaliah's slaying,[46] they gathered themselves to a place called Geruth Chimham, near Bethlehem, to make plans to migrate to Egypt (41:16-18).

  2. *Migration to Egypt* (42:1—43:7)

  a. *Jeremiah's Counsel Sought* (42:1-6). The first actions and deliberation of the Jews and their leaders in their conference as to what move to make, had every appearance of assuring success:

1) They were of one accord: "from the least even unto the greatest" (42:1).

2) They asked a man of God to pray for them: "Pray for us unto Jehovah thy God" (42:2).

3) They recognized their impotence: "we are left but a few of many" (42:2).

4) They sought directions: "wherein we should walk" (42:3).

5) They would obey God's direction: "whether it be

---

[46]Is the deportation referred to in 52:30 such a reprisal?

106

good, or whether it be evil, we will obey the voice of Jehovah our God" (42:6).

Ten days later God gave Jeremiah the answer.[47] The essence of the message was that the remnant of Judah must remain in the land, not fearing Nebuchadrezzar, but trusting God for protection (42:10-12). To go to Egypt would bring the sword and famine (42:13-22).

b. Nebuchadrezzar's Vengeance Feared (43:1-7). How quickly promises are broken! Contrary to their original promise, the leaders and the people did not accept Jeremiah's answer as coming from Jehovah, attributing it rather to Baruch's contriving. Not trusting God for protection, they feared death at the hands of Nebuchadrezzar (43:1-3). And thus began the journey to Egypt of all the remnant—men, women, children, the king's daughters, "and Jeremiah . . . and Baruch" (43:5-6)—the latter two going, undoubtedly, against their hearts' desires. The journey was apparently uneventful; eventually they arrived at the city of Tahpanhes (43:7).[48] Ironically, in a previous century Israel had pleaded to God to be delivered from Egypt; now a remnant disobeyed God in seeking a home in that very land.

3. *Judgment of the Refugees* (43:8—44:30)

Soon after arriving at Tahpanhes, God gave Jeremiah more details as to the future judgment of both Egypt and the Jewish refugees who had now settled in the land against His will.

a. Jeremiah's Prophecy Declared (43:8—44:14). Jere-

---

[47]This is a vital lesson in the prayer life of the Christian. God's answer, yes *or* no, will not come until *His* time; and who knows how many days will intervene!

[48]Tahpanhes was on the eastern border of the delta of Egypt, on the road from Egypt to Palestine.

miah was directed of God to bury large stones "in mortar under the pavement" (Berkeley Version) at the entry of Pharaoh's house, telling the men of Judah that this symbolized the impending fate of Egypt, namely, that its throne would be subjugated to that of Nebuchadrezzar, who would set his royal pavilion over the Egyptian pavement (43:8-10). He would also smite the people utterly, breaking down their idols (43:11-13). Egypt would be as closely identified with this throne as a man's garments are with his frame (43:12).[49]

The message of 43:8-13 had to do with the fate of Egypt. Now Jeremiah was told by God what would be the fate of "the Jews that dwelt in the land of Egypt" (44:1). God reminded the refugees of the idolatry of Jerusalem and the other cities of Judah and the consequential judgment of His wrath (44:2-6). The Jews in Egypt had been guilty of the same sins, "burning incense unto other gods in the land of Egypt" (44:7-10); therefore they too must reap God's judgment, all but a remnant being consumed in the land of their flight (44:11-14).

b. *Refugees' Challenge Given* (44:15-19). The Jews challenged Jeremiah's interpretation of the judgment. In one voice[50] they rejected Jeremiah's word for their own (44:16-17). Whereas Jeremiah cited Jerusalem's destruc-

---

[49]It is not known when during Nebuchadrezzar's reign this prophecy was entirely fulfilled, though an ancient inscription states that he did later invade Egypt (568 B.C.) and overthrow it. There is no reason to deny that Nebuchadrezzar did conquer Egypt. "The fact that this prophecy was left in this book by the next generation argues for knowledge on their part (now lost to us) of a reduction of the land by Nebuchadnezzar" (Pfeiffer and Harrison, *op. cit.*, p. 686).

[50]Note the all-inclusive phrases of 44:15: "all the men," "all the women," and "all the people."

tion as being the punitive action of God, they interpreted it as being the wrath of the "queen of heaven" for discontinuing offerings to her, which was one of the reformation purges under Josiah. "For then [in prereformation days] had we plenty. . . . But since we left off burning incense to the queen of heaven . . . we have wanted all things (44:17-18).

c. Refugees' Doom Sealed (44:20-30). These are the last prophetic words of Jeremiah to be recorded in his book.[51] The prophet reasserts the true reason for the Jews' judgment (44:20-23), and adds a few new facts or emphases to his prophetic message:

1) God's name would "no more be named in the mouth of any man of Judah in all the land of Egypt" (44:26).[52]

2) The Jews in Egypt would know whose word would stand—"mine, or theirs" (44:28).

3) The sign of God's judgment against the Jews was given in the prophecy of the fate of Egypt's Pharaoh Hophra, who would be assassinated by his enemies.[53]

* * *

It is very significant that the last recorded words of Jeremiah should contain the challenge of God to all other voices that have refused His prophet:

---

[51]The prophecies of the succeeding chapters were spoken at earlier times.

[52]The temporal phrase "no more" very likely referred to the era in which the words were spoken, not intending to refer to a later era, such as the intertestamental period, when there was a large segment of Jews in Egypt. Or, the prophecy may have had a conditional character about it. See Pfeiffer and Harrison, *loc. cit.*

[53]Pharaoh Hophra reigned as king of Egypt 588-569 B.C. One of his officials, Amasis, succeeded him, and was later his assassin (564 B.C.).

"[They] shall know whose word shall stand,
MINE, OR THEIRS" (44:28*b*).

All the conflicts of the world today can be summed up in the one critical conflict: *The word of man vs. the Word of God*. Because the word of man has its source in corruptness, it is impotent in its attempts to destroy the bulwark of God's incorruptible Word. In the last of the judgments, every unbeliever shall acknowledge God's Word to be the truth.

* * *

What went through the mind of the aged and weary prophet as he walked the streets of Tahpanhes, recalling the indelible past? Surely he thought of the day God called him to the divine task, and of the subsequent years of preaching His unpopular message to a hostile audience. Those were lonely years, and trying ones. But he fought a good fight, and now the course was finished. Soon he would meet God face to face, receive rewards, and enter into blessed eternal fellowship with Him.

The book of Jeremiah does not record the last days of the prophet, even as the book of Acts lets the Apostle Paul fade out of its narrative. The intention of such an ending to the books must be, among other things, to emphasize the blessed truth that though in a sense one's earthly ministry comes to a close, its fruits continue in time and eternity. Consider the uninterrupted ministries of Jeremiah and Paul to this day. What Christian is not indebted to both men of God, who, for the fire in their bones, could not but speak the Word committed to them?

110

THE SUPPLEMENTS TO THE BOOK OF JEREMIAH

(45:1—52:34)

THE MESSAGE of the recorded prophecies of Jeremiah has formally concluded. Placed at the end of the book are three sections which appear to be supplements to the main body of the prophecy, each of which is reserved to the last pages for a different purpose.

I. GOD'S MESSAGE TO BARUCH (45:1-5)

This chapter, dated in the fourth year of Jehoiakim, could be placed chronologically after 36:1-8, but the theme of the latter-mentioned section is centered about the *scroll* of prophecy, not about its *scribe*, Baruch. Hence this chapter (45) of Baruch's personal reactions to his commission is reserved to this supplementary section.

Baruch, though only the professional recorder of the scroll of Jeremiah's prophecy, could not help but become emotionally involved with the oppressive message of doom: "I am weary with my groaning" (45:3). For his complaint, God's rebuke was brief and sharp, though not without grace:

1) Acknowledge My sovereign will as concerns judgment (45:4).

2) Do not selfishly seek great things for yourself (45:5*a*).

3) You are one of the few whom I will spare in the judgment (45:5*b*).

II. GOD'S MESSAGE TO THE FOREIGN NATIONS (46:1—51:64)

Besides being a prophet to his own brethren, Jeremiah was called of God to be "a prophet unto the nations" (1:5).[1] This section describes the prophecies of God's judgments against Judah's neighboring nations for their sin. From a topical and chronological standpoint, the section could have been placed in connection with 25:15 ff.[2] But since the main thrust of Jeremiah's total prophecy concerned Judah, its placement there would have effected a considerable parenthesis. Furthermore, the fulfillment of the prophecies regarding the evil nations was to come *after* the destruction of Jerusalem, hence their placement here at the end of the book is very appropriate from that standpoint.

The order in which the oracles are recorded follows a general geographical pattern of *west to east,* as the following diagram indicates:[3]

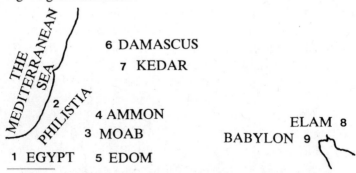

6 DAMASCUS

7 KEDAR

4 AMMON

ELAM 8

3 MOAB

BABYLON 9

1 EGYPT   5 EDOM

[1]Compare the similar ministries of Amos (Amos 1:3—2:5); Isaiah (Isa. 13-23); and Ezekiel (Ezek. 25-32).

[2]The Septuagint Version places it after 25:13. The foreign-nation oracle of chapter 25 states in condensed form what chapters 46 through 51 elaborate.

[3]The location of Kedar is approximate, since the name represents various nomadic tribes of the area.

The oracles against the nations were intended mainly to describe the judgments rather than identify the sins which were their causes. Hence some oracles made no mention of sins. The conqueror of the fallen nation is not always cited, though in such prophecies the Chaldean army is the unnamed power. In the case of Babylon itself, the "nations from the north" (50:9) are identified as Medes (51:11), Ararat, Minni, and Ashkenaz (51:27), kingdoms which were located to the north of Chaldea. A future restoration is explicitly stated for Egypt, Moab, Ammon, and Elam. (See chart on pages 114-115.)

III. THE FALL OF JERUSALEM (52:1-34)

The concluding verse of chapter 51 states explicitly that the words preceding it "are the words of Jeremiah" (51:64*b*). Whether or not this precludes Jeremiahic authorship of chapter 52,[5] it does confirm what the content of chapter 51 indicates, that this last chapter of the book of Jeremiah stands by itself as an addendum.[6]

The chapter very appropriately concludes the prophecy for these reasons: (1) the fall of Jerusalem is the crucial fulfillment of the book's prophecy, and (2) the postscript-like reference to Jehoiachin's release from prison illustrates the fact that the judgments prophesied were totally destructive in their scope.

---

[5]See Carl F. Keil and Franz Delitzsch, *The Prophecies of Jeremiah* (Grand Rapids: Wm. B. Erdmans Publishing Co., 1950), II, 322-23, also Philip Schaff (ed.), "Jeremiah," *Lange's Commentary on the Holy Scriptures* (Grand Rapids: Zondervan Pub. House, n.d.), VI, 436-37, for a discussion of the authorship of chapter 52.

[6]Its contents are practically identical to those of II Kings 24:18 ff.; 25:21, 27-30.

The following is a tabulation of the general contents of
the nine oracles of chapters 46 through 51:

NATION	PASSAGE	JUDGMENTS	SINS	CONQUEROR	FUTURE RESTORATION
Egypt	46:2-12	army of Egypt to fall (at Carchemish)⁴	none listed	Nebuchadrezzar, 46:13	46:26 (cf. Ezek. 29:13-14)
	46:13-26	land of Egypt to be smitten			
Philistines	chap. 47	to be destroyed	none listed	from the North, 47:2	
Moab	chap. 48	utter destruction and desolation	1. trusting in works, 48:7 2. self-magnification, 48:26,42 3. opposing Israel, 48:27 4. pride and arrogance, 48:29	not identified	48:47, "latter days"

Ammon	49:1-6	desolation and captivity	1. opposing Israel, 49:2 2. trusting in wealth, 49:4	not identified	49:6
Edom	49:7-22	desolation	pride, 49:16	not identified	
Damascus	49:23-27	wasting by fire	none listed	not identified	
Kedar and Hazor	49:28-33	scattering and desolation	none listed	Nebuchadrezzar, 49:30	
Elam	49:34-39	scattering and destruction	none listed	not identified	49:39, "latter days"
Babylon	50:1— 51:64	annihilation, never to rise again, 51:64	1. idolatry, 50:2; 51:47,52 2. "striving against Jehovah," 50:24 3. pride, 50:29	nations from the North, 50:9,41; 51:11,27 ff.	

¹Fulfilled at the Battle of Carchemish in 605 B.C.

The main items found in chapter 52 which are not recorded in chapter 39 are:

1) summary statement of Zedekiah's reign and sin (52:1-3)

2) list of the temple objects destroyed or confiscated (52:17-23)

3) identification of some of Judah's leaders taken captive (52:24-25)

4) the three deportations of Nebuchadrezzar (52:28-30):

DEPORTATION	YEAR OF JERUSALEM'S SIEGE	RULER OF JERUSALEM	CAPTIVES TAKEN
FIRST	7th (597)	Jehoiachin	3,023[7]
SECOND	18th (586)	Zedekiah	832
THIRD	23rd (581)	Governor Gedaliah	4,600[8]

5) Jehoiachin's release from prison (52:31-34)

---

[7]See II Kings 24:12-16. It has been suggested that the 10,000 captives of II Kings may refer to how many were taken at Jerusalem; the smaller number of Jeremiah 52:28 may be the number arriving at Babylon.

[8]There is no other Bible reference to this third deportation. Some have suggested that this took place as a retaliation for the slaying of Gedaliah (41:2). See Charles F. Pfeiffer and Everett F. Harrison (eds.), *The Wycliffe Bible Commentary* (Chicago: Moody Press, 1962), p. 693.

116

LAMENTATIONS

INTRODUCTION

LAMENTATIONS is an appropriate sequel to the book of Jeremiah, for it looks back to the same event which Jeremiah anticipated: the fall of Jerusalem, 586 B.C.

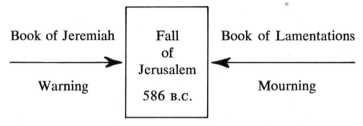

Book of Jeremiah	Fall of Jerusalem 586 B.C.	Book of Lamentations
Warning		Mourning

Knowing from Jeremiah's prophecies how he wept over his people before judgment fell, it is not difficult for us to imagine the depths to which his soul sank in utter grief as he watched the holy city burning and his people being ravished. Lamentations reveals something of the pathos of that experience. It is the Bible's classic book on grief over judgment. Delbert Hillers writes:

> Lamentations served the survivors of the catastrophe in the first place as an expression of the almost inexpressible horror and grief they felt. Men live on best, after calamity, not by utterly repressing their grief and shock, but by facing it, by measuring its dimensions, by finding some form of words to order and articulate their experience. Lamentations is so complete and honest and elo-

quent an expression of grief that even centuries after the events which inspired it, it is still able to provide those in mute despair with words to speak.[1]

We shall see later that Lamentations is more than a book of grief: confession and hope are two of its bright lights.

Historical Background

Before we come to the text of Lamentations, let us consider its background and history.

Title. Hebrew Bibles use either of two titles for the book: (1) *Ekhah* ("Ah, how," or, "Alas"); this is the opening Hebrew word of chapters 1, 2, and 4, (2) *Qinoth* (lamentations); the writer laments the destruction of Jerusalem.

Greek Bibles, such as the Septuagint version, have used the title *Threnoi* (lamentations, from *threomai,* to cry aloud). This was carried over into the Latin Bibles as *Liber Threnorum* (Book of Lamentations), and thence into the English Bibles as Lamentations.

Place in the Old Testament Canon. In the threefold Hebrew Bible (Law, Prophets, Writings), Lamentations appears in the last part, in a section called "Megilloth." The Megilloth is a group of five Old Testament books which the Jews read publicly on national holidays. Lamentations is read on the ninth day of Ab (about mid-July), the anniversary of the destructions of Jerusalem in 586 B.C. and A.D. 70.

In some ancient versions of the Bible, Lamentations appeared as an appendix to Jeremiah and often was not included in the listing of the Old Testament books. In our English Bible, the book very appropriately follows Jeremiah's prophecy, in view of its message.

[1]Delbert R. Hillers, *Lamentations* (Garden City, N.Y.: Doubleday, 1972), p. xvi.

Author and date. Lamentations was very likely written soon after 586 B.C., while memories of the appalling siege of Jerusalem were still fresh. Some think that the author wrote chapter 5 a little later than the first four chapters, "when the intense anguish of the catastrophe had given way to the prolonged ache of captivity."[2]

As to authorship, the evidence points strongly, though not conclusively, to Jeremiah.[3] Such evidence includes the following: (1) the Septuagint and Vulgate introductions to the book, which read in part: "Jeremiah sat weeping and lamented with this lamentation over Jerusalem, and said—", (2) Hebrew and Gentile tradition, (3) similarities between Lamentations and poetical portions of Jeremiah (cf. also II Chron. 35:25)[4], (4) the writer was an eyewitness of Jerusalem's destruction, with a sensitivity of soul (cf. Jer. 9:1; 14:17-22) and an ability to write.

Composition and Style. Lamentations is a set of five elegies (melancholy poems), written in a mournful style.[5] The rhythm of the lines in the original Hebrew is described as a "limping meter," wherein the second of two parallel parts is one beat shorter than the first. When the Hebrew words of 1:1 are carried over exactly into English, one can see this limping meter (here, three sounds followed by two, in Hebrew):

[2]D. A. Hubbard, "Book of Lamentations," in *The New Bible Dictionary,* p. 707. If Jeremiah was the author, it would be better to describe his experience as "exile" (in Egypt), rather than "captivity" (cf. Jer. 43).

[3]Arguments for and against Jeremiah's authorship are extensively developed in Lange's commentary on Lamentations, pp. 6-16 and 19-35.

[4]See Edward J. Young, *Introduction to the Old Testament,* pp. 333-336.

[5]It is unfortunate that all Bible editions do not print this book in the format of poetry.

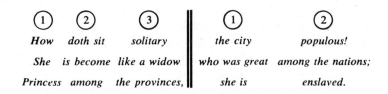

	①	②	③	‖	①	②
	How	*doth sit*	*solitary*	‖	*the city*	*populous!*
	She	*is become*	*like a widow*	‖	*who was great*	*among the nations;*
	Princess	*among*	*the provinces,*	‖	*she is*	*enslaved.*

When read publicly, the chanting of the Hebrew text gave support to the mood of the words.

One of the distinctive features of the book is the acrostic format of chapters 1-4.[6] In chapters 1, 2, and 4 each verse begins with a word whose first letter is successively one of the twenty-two letters of the Hebrew alphabet. Chapter 3 has sixty-six verses, each successive letter of the alphabet having three verses allotted to it instead of one. If the acrostic format had been used in the English versions, the chapters might read like this, showing the English alphabet:[7]

CHAP. 1 (sixty-six lines, twenty-two verses)
    v. 1: Ah!

            _____

            _____

    v. 2: Bitterly she weeps

            _____

            _____

    v. 3: Captive is Judah

            _____

            _____

[6]Psalm 119 is a classic example of acrostic writing.

[7]The paraphrases shown are intended only to illustrate the acrostic device. They are not recommended as translations.

CHAP. 2 (sixty-six lines, twenty-two verses) similar to chap. 1

CHAP. 3 (sixty-six lines, sixty-six verses)
v. 1: Affliction by the rod
v. 2: And in darkness, not in light
v. 3: All the day
v. 4: Bones of mine
v. 5: Bitterness and distress
v. 6: Buried in dark places

CHAP. 4 (forty-four lines, twenty-two verses)
v. 1: Ah, how

———————————————

v. 2: Belittled

———————————————

CHAP. 5 (forty-four lines, twenty-two verses) not an acrostic

Various views are held as to why the author used this acrostic device. Among them are: (1) as an aid to memorization, (2) as a symbol of the *fullness* of the people's grief (i.e., from A to Z), (3) to confine the expression of boundless grief by the limiting device of an acrostic.

Message. Lamentations is a book of doom and hope. It expresses grief over judgment, confession of sin, recognition of the Lord's holiness and glory, and pleas for mercy. The book does not intend to give the impression that the Israelites as a nation did confess their sin and turn to God while being taken captive by the Chaldeans. Whenever Jeremiah attributes such redemptive words to the people (e.g., 5:21), he does so in an idealistic and evangelistic

123

sense. The burden of his heart, even as before captivity, was that out of judgment the people *would* turn to God. Only God knows to what extent this book was circulated among the Jews immediately after it was written, doing its intended ministry of reconciliation.

One can see why the message of Lamentations is so contemporary. Ross Price comments on this:

> Protestant Christians, one regrets to say, have too often neglected the reading of these solemn poems. Yet in these days of personal, national, and international crises (and disaster) the message of this book is a challenge to repent of sins personal, national, and international, and to commit ourselves afresh to God's steadfast love. Though this love is everpresent and outgoing, a holy and just God must surely judge unrepentant sinners.[8]

Christ in the Book of Lamentations. The many references to the Lord ("Jehovah") in the book of Lamentations may be applied today to the ministry of Jesus Christ. This is because the works of God the Father are one with the works of His Son. For example, when we read, "It is of Jehovah's lovingkindnesses that we are not consumed" (3:22), we may rightly say, "It is of Christ's mercies that we are not consumed" (cf. Jude 21).

There are some descriptions of Israel in Lamentations which, while not intended to be predictive of Christ's ministry, do represent, picture-wise, different aspects of that ministry.[9] Among these are Christ as (1) the afflicted of

---

[8]Ross Price, "Lamentations," *The Wycliffe Bible Commentary*, p. 696. The religious calendars of the Jewish and Catholic faiths assign the reading of the book once a year. For the latter, it is read on the last three days of Holy Week.

[9]Care should be exercised in this area of application. In the words of Norman Geisler, "Any Old Testament passage may be appropriately applied to Christ, even though the New Testament writers did not apply

the Lord (1:12), (2) despised of His enemies (2:15-16), (3) derision to all the people (3:14), (4) the smitten and insulted One (3:30), (5) the weeping Prophet (cf. Matt. 23:37-38).

Survey of Lamentations

A scanning of the book of Lamentations reveals the following, among other things:

1. The book has five chapters, each of which is a separate poem.
2. Sometimes Jeremiah speaks for himself ("I"); sometimes the Jewish captives (including Jeremiah) speak ("We"); and sometimes Jeremiah writes about his brethren ("They").
3. The prevailing tone is utter grief and resignation. At a few places, a ray of hope shines through. Such hope is brightest in the middle of chapter 3.
4. There is much imagery in the book (e.g., "From on high hath he sent fire into my bones," 1:13).
5. Short prayers to God appear from time to time. The entire last chapter is a prayer.
6. Jeremiah continually acknowledges God's holiness, justice and sovereignty in the judgments which He has sent upon Judah.
7. References to the people's sins appear from time to time in the book.
8. The book ends on a note of hope (5:19-22).[10]

it, providing that it exemplifies something from the life of the Messianic people which finds an actual correspondence with the truth about Christ presented somewhere in the Bible" (Norman Geisler, *Christ: The Theme of the Bible* [Chicago: Moody Press, 1968], p. 65).

[10]Though the last verse expresses despair, an alternate reading supports the optimism of v. 21. This will be discussed further in the commentary section.

LAMENTATIONS   THE SINNER MOURNS OVER HIS AFFLICTIONS

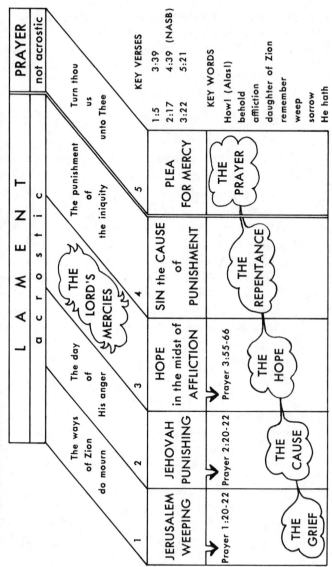

	L A M E N T				PRAYER
	a c r o s t i c				not acrostic
	The ways of Zion do mourn	The day of His anger		The punishment of the iniquity	Turn thou us unto Thee
	1	2	3	4	5
	JERUSALEM WEEPING	JEHOVAH PUNISHING	HOPE in the midst of AFFLICTION	SIN the CAUSE of PUNISHMENT	PLEA FOR MERCY
	Prayer 1:20-22	Prayer 2:20-22	Prayer 3:55-66		
	THE GRIEF	THE CAUSE	THE HOPE	THE REPENTANCE	THE PRAYER

THE LORD'S MERCIES

KEY VERSES

1:5   3:39
2:17   4:39 (NASB)
3:22   5:21

KEY WORDS

Howl (Alas!)
behold
affliction
daughter of Zion
remember
weep
sorrow
He hath

126

2. *Fallen Jerusalem Laments* (1:12-19)

Now Jeremiah changes the third person "she" to first person "I" in the elegy, because he wants the Israelites to express their own inner feelings by way of testimony. The use of the singular "I" instead of the plural "we" makes the testimony individualized. This is right, for while the people suffered as a group, their deepest grief was personal and individual.

The stanza opens and closes on the same note: that of groaning, moaning, and self-pity (1:12, 22b). The captive cries for all the affliction which has come upon him (1:12-16a). But the sharpest hurt is that "the comforter that should refresh my soul is far from me" (1:16). This is, in fact, the reason for the opening complaint, "Is it nothing to you, all ye that pass by?" (1:12). And the author inserts the parenthesis of 1:17 to say the same thing: "Zion spreadeth forth her hands; there is none to comfort her" (1:17). In 1:18a the captive anticipates the charge that he deserves his judgment, and so he confesses his own guilt and acknowledges God to be righteous. But, he persists, Hear me now, all you peoples, and behold my suffering 1:18b, Berkeley).

Perhaps the most pathetic cry of the captive is the one ed above, "The comforter that should refresh my soul ar from me" (1:16). If that absent comforter was God, some interpret the text,[2] the words prepare the reader the captive's prayer to God recorded in 1:20-22. Truly all-sufficient comforter to one who has been punished od must be God Himself.

"The Lamentations of Jeremiah," in *Lange's Commentary on the 'criptures*, 12:56. Also see the paraphrase of 1:16 in *The Living*

The accompanying survey chart shows the general pattern of Lamentations' five chapters.

Note the following on the chart:

1. The first four chapters are dirges, written in acrostic style. Chapter 5 is basically a prayer; and it is non-acrostic.
2. The middle chapter (3) is the brightest. Various references to the Lord's mercies are made here.
3. There is a natural progression of thought throughout the chapters. In chapter 1 the prophet and people are weeping over Jerusalem's destruction; in chapter 2 God's judgments, as the cause of the grief, are described; chapter 3 shows where hope is to be found; in chapter 4 sin is acknowledged as the cause of divine judgment; and in chapter 5 the prophet prays in behalf of his brethren as he pleads for God's deliverance.
4. Chapters 1-3 each end with a prayer; chapter 4 is an exception, and chapter 5 is also a prayer.
5. A few selected key words are listed on the chart. Read the key verses which are cited.

BOOK OF LAMENTATIONS

I. LAMENT (1:1—4:22)

A. Jerusalem Weeps (1:1-22)

All five poems of Lamentations express the grief of captive Jerusalem, but in this first one, the weeping and lamenting are most prominent.[1] This is suggested by the following words and phrases which appear throughout the poem: "weepeth sore," "tears," "mourn," "bitterness," "affliction," "miseries," "sigheth," "sorrow," "mine eye runneth down with water," "distress."

1. *Fallen Jerusalem Described* (1:1-11)

The prophet speaks of Jerusalem as a "widow" (1:___) and so throughout the stanza the city is referred to by ___ pronoun "she." She is described as being solitary, ___tary, comfortless, captive, afflicted, desolate, and ___ despised. One cannot help but feel that the proph___ a loss to adequately express the state of Israel at th___ The phrase, "she has fallen astonishingly" (1:9, ___ is bluntly paraphrased in *The Living Bible* as, "___ lies in the gutter."

At least three times in this stanza the sin of ___ ites is acknowledged: (1) "Jehovah hath afflic___ the multitude of her transgressions" (1:5), (2) ___ hath grievously sinned" (1:8), (3) "Her filt___ her skirts" (1:9).

Also prominent in the verses are two sho___ when fallen Jerusalem cries out to the Lord ___ O Jehovah, my affliction; for the enemy ___ himself" (1:9), (2) "See, O LORD, and ___ despised" (1:11, NASB). As noted ea___ miah's burden that the Jewish captive___ the Lord for help.

---

[1] Stanza divisions are at vv. 1, 12, 20.

3. *Plea for Vindication* (1:20-22)

The Jews wanted to "remind" God that their Babylonian captors were also sinners, deserving of God's judgment: "Let all their wickedness come before thee; And do unto them, as thou hast done unto me for all my transgressions" (1:22). (Read the verse aloud, putting the emphasis on the appropriate words.) It was an appeal for justice and equity, the performance of which would alleviate their distress and bring at least a measure of comfort.

But Jeremiah did not want the Jews to rest their case with that plea for equity. They as sinners deserved their judgment, and hope lay only in the mercy of God. Hence the prophet has them speaking the opening words of 1:20: "Look on, O LORD, for I am in distress" (Berkeley). Here, as repentant Jewish captives, they are appealing to the mercy and grace of God for their own deliverance. If only He would look down upon them, and have mercy!

B. Jehovah Punishes (2:1-22)

This poem may be divided into four stanzas,[3] shown in the accompanying diagram.

1	10	13	20 22
Jeremiah speaking			Zion speaking
The Lord's punishments	The consequences	Reflections, and exhortations to Zion	Lament to God
①	②	③	④

[3]Stanza divisions are at vv. 1, 10, 13, and 20. V. 9, instead of v. 10, could be the beginning of that new stanza.

131

1. *Punishments Described* (2:1-9)

The key repeated phrase throughout the stanza is "He hath." There are about forty descriptions of divine judgment, which fell upon every aspect of the Jews' life: home, religion, society, physical, mental and spiritual. Some of the blackest phrases of the book appear here, such as: "he hath poured out his wrath like fire" (2:4c), "The Lord is become an enemy" (2:5), and "her prophets find no vision from Jehovah" (2:9).

2. *The Consequences* (2:10-12)

Now Jeremiah describes a few pathetic scenes—of silenced elders, shamed virgins, and starved children. He is a broken man for what he has seen: "I have cried until the tears no longer come; my heart is broken, my spirit poured out, as I see what has happened to my people" (2: 11a, TLB).

3. *The Prophet's Reflections, and Exhortations to Zion* (2:13-19)

In these seven verses, Jeremiah addresses his Jewish brethren, whom he calls "daughter of Jerusalem" and "virgin daughter of Zion" (2:13). After lamenting what the Lord has done to Jerusalem, he exhorts the Jews to cry unto the Lord for help: "Pour out thy heart like water before the face of the Lord" (2:19). The next stanza records their prayer.

4. *Zion's Lament to God* (2:20-22)

This concluding stanza is a prayer to God, as its opening words indicate. But it is basically a complaint, spoken in a very bitter tone. The only redemptive note is found in the first line, where there is a faint suggestion of a plea for mercy, similar to that of 1:20a: "See, O Jehovah, and behold to whom thou hast done thus!" (2:20; cf. 3:50). Perhaps when Jeremiah composed this stanza, he was realistically representing the captives' feelings but also suggesting a small step upward out of the slough of despair.

C. Hope in the Midst of Affliction (3:1-66)

This middle poem of Lamentations[4] could be called the high peak of the book, because the brightest and most hopeful things are written here. The title of one of our grand hymns comes from the heart of the poem, "Great is thy faithfulness" (3:23). It is interesting to observe that just as a man's hope arises out of a dark experience, so in the poem the stanza about hope is surrounded by two stanzas about affliction.

1. *The Suffering Servant* (3:1-18)

The first four words, *I am the man,* alert the reader that what follows involves the author personally. Of all the stanzas of the book which are written with the pronoun "I," this one is most clearly the personal testimony of the author.[5] Ross Price comments:

> Here Jeremiah bares his heart to the reader. . . . His life was one long martyrdom, in which he served as both judge and intercessor for people bent on their own destruction. No prophet ever pleaded with a people in more impassioned manner, calling for a national conversion, than did he. And no one, except Jesus, was treated with more national contempt than he. [Cf. Isa. 53 and Psa. 22.][6]

The prophet's testimony is utter dejection because he is looking at his mission to Israel as a failure. Here is how he

---

[4]Stanza divisions are at vv. 1, 19, 43, 55.

[5]At the same time, Jeremiah is speaking here as the representative of his captive brethren.

[6]Ross Price, "Lamentations," in *The Wycliffe Bible Commentary,* p. 698.

expresses some of his experiences: "He [God] hath led me and caused me to walk in darkness" (3:2), "He shutteth out my prayer" (3:8), "I am become a derision to all my people" (3:14), "Mine expectation from Jehovah [is perished]" (3:18). These were despairing words, but at least the prophet was honest.

2. *Hope in the Lord* (3:19-42)

Quickly Jeremiah wants to say that he has found hope, and that the hope is in the Lord. A free paraphrase of 3:21-22 is, "I have hope when I remind myself that it is because of the Lord's mercies that we are not consumed."[7] Line after line expands on this bright theme. Consider these: "His compassions . . . are new every morning" (3:22-23), "Great is thy faithfulness" (3:23), "Jehovah is good unto them that wait for him" (3:25), "The Lord will not cast off for ever" (3:31), "He doth not afflict willingly" (3:33).

The stanza concludes on what an afflicted person should *not* do: "Why should any living mortal, or any man, Offer complaint in view of his sins?" (3:39, NASB); and what he *should* do: "Let us search and try our ways, and turn again to Jehovah" (3:40).

3. *The Suffering Nation* (3:43-54)

For some reason, the author returns to the theme of affliction, just as night returns after the daylight. The persecutions of the nation (3:43-48) as well as of the prophet (3:49-54) are cited. There is one bright star in the night—the line of verse 50: "till Jehovah look down, and behold from heaven." The key words are in the opening lines of some of the prophet's earlier prayers. (See 1:9, 11, 20; 2:20.)

[7]See also the Berkeley translation of these verses.

4. *Prayer of Gratitude* (3:55-66)

The opening lines are the prominent ones, even though the prayer ends on a severe note of imprecation. The tone is one of deep gratitude to the Lord for hearing the prophet when he called upon Him out of the dungeon of despair and affliction. No greater testimony can a sinner offer to God than to say, in thanksgiving, "Thou hast redeemed my life" (3:58).

D. Sin the Cause of Punishment (4:1-22)

In the poem of chapter 3,[8] Jeremiah reached the mountain peak of hope—the mercy of the Lord. The next two poems show that sinful man can appropriate the blessings of that hope by (1) acknowledging and repenting of sin, and (2) turning to the Lord for salvation. Chapter 4 is the acknowledgment of sin, and chapter 5 is the prayer of salvation. Compare this combination with the effectual prayer of the publican, which Jesus commended, "God, be thou merciful to me a sinner" (Luke 18:13).[9]

1. *Horrors of the Siege* (4:1-12)

The siege of Jerusalem was devastating, and the consequences tragic. The punishment even exceeded that brought upon the inhabitants of Sodom for their sin (4:6). The lines of this stanza compare Jerusalem before and after the siege, and every picture is dark, sometimes repulsive (cf. 4:10). Even gold, that supposedly changeless commodity, has changed! (4:1). The success of the Chaldean invaders is the headline of the century: "The kings of the earth, and all the inhabitants of the world, would not have believed that the adversary and the enemy [could] have entered into the gates of Jerusalem" (4:12, KJV).

[8]Stanza divisions are at verses 1, 13, and 21.
[9]See also II Ch. 7:14.

2. *Sin as the Cause* (4:13-20)

The recurring main point of this stanza is that Israel's sin brought on her punishment. Jeremiah could have cited many kinds of iniquity committed by the people, but he singled out two glaring examples: (1) the corruption of Israel's spiritual leaders—prophets and priests (4:13-16),[10] (2) the people's trust in man ("we have watched shadow[12] we shall live among the nations," 4:20).

3. *A Ray of Hope* (4:21-22)

In the previous stanza, the people had bewailed what looked like their irrecoverable and hopeless lot: "Our end is near, our days are fulfilled; for our end is come" (4:18). In these last two verses, however, Judah is consoled by two facts: (1) Judah is not alone in judgment. For example, Edom would also be punished for her sin (4:21, 22*b*[13], (2) Judah's captivity will eventually come to an end (4:22*a*). This prophecy had been revealed to the prophet by God.

Chapter 4 does not end with a prayer, as do the preceding chapters, but it is followed by a prayer—all of chapter 5.

II. PRAYER (5:1-22)

The best fruit of anyone's mourning is his praying to

[10]This was a common theme of Jeremiah's preaching, as recorded in the following passages: Jeremiah 6:13; 8:10; 14:14-16; 23:9-40.

for a nation[11] that could not save," 4:17; "under his

[11]Read Jeremiah 37:3-10 for the story of Judah's dependence on Egypt.

[12]This is a reference to Judah's King Zedekiah, whose fate is described in Jeremiah 52:8-11.

[13]The Edomites were descended from Edom, whose other name was Esau (Gen 25:30; 36:1). Esau was the brother of Jacob, a father of the Jewish people. Thus the nation of Edom was kin to the nation of Judah, though the two were constant enemies. The phrase "Rejoice and be glad, O daughter of Edom" (4:21) may be a reference to Edom's gloating over her own safety while Jerusalem was being besieged.

136

God. Since the concluding poem of Lamentations is that kind of a prayer,[14] it is correct to say that the book ends on a high note. We have seen earlier that chapter 3 was a high peak of the book, with its many references to the goodness and mercy of God. But the real test for the captive Jews was whether they would appropriate that mercy and turn to the Lord. Chapter 5 is the prayer of the captive who passed the test.

A. "Look Upon Us" (5:1-10)

Throughout the stanza, Judah bewails its affliction, not so much for the sheer sake of complaint,[15] but to move God to consider their plight. Here are the familiar words of earlier prayers, "Behold, and see our reproach" (5:1).

B. "Woe Unto Us" (5:11-18)

Now the people relate their affliction to just deserts for sin and cry out, "Woe unto us! for we have sinned" (5:16). A few moments earlier, they had bewailed having to reap consequences of their fathers' sins (5:7; cf. Ex 20:5); now they acknowledge that God has sent judgment for their own sins (cf. Ezek 8:1-4).

One of the most pathetic lines in the book of Lamentations is 5:15a, "The joy of our heart is ceased." The timeless, universal truth taught here is that sin dispels true joy.

C. "Turn Thou Us" (5:19-22)

The concluding stanza of Lamentations is of four parts:

14Stanza divisions are at vv. 1, 11, 19. Note: the literary style of chap. 5 is different from the preceding chapters in at least two ways: (1) it is not an acrostic, and (2) its lines are much shorter.

15Verse 7, however, suggests a complaining mood. (See the paraphrase in *The Living Bible*.)

1. *Ascription* (v. 19)

   The eternal character of the Lord's throne is recognized and praised. (Earthly thrones topple all too quickly, as the Jews had experienced!)

2. *Question* (v. 20)

   "Why do You forsake us for so long?" implies "Since Your throne abides forever, You won't forget us forever, will you?"

3. *Petition* (v. 21)

   "Turn thou us unto thee, O Jehovah," is the heart's crucial prayer of conversion.

4. *Question* (v. 22)

   "Or hast thou utterly rejected us?" implies "Surely you won't reject us for ever!"[16]

The full force of the ascription (v. 19) and petition (v. 21) is felt when the other two verses are interpreted as implied statements (shown above). In any case, the prominent verse is the prayer of conversion (v. 21), about which one writer comments, "Suffering has done its work, the prodigal has come to himself and is ready to arise and go to his Father."[17]

* * *

If Jeremiah was the author of Lamentations, the book is clearly a testimony of how godly the prophet remained to the very end of his ministry. When the Jews were taken captive, he might have reveled in an attitude of "I told you so." But that was not Jeremiah. He continued to weep for

[16]The Revised Standard Version, along with other translations, prefers to read the text as a question, which is allowable. It is interesting to note that today when Jews read publicly the text of Lamentations, they read v. 22 before v. 21, so that the concluding note is not despairing. They do the same for the last verse of Malachi.

[17]L. E. H. Stephens-Hodge, "Lamentations," in *The New Bible Commentary*, p. 644.

the souls of his people, and Lamentations shows us how he exhorted them in their tribulation. Only God knows how many Jews, of those who had scorned his preaching before captivity, now came into the fold of a believing remnant by praying the prayer of 5:21, "Turn thou us unto thee, O Jehovah, and we shall be turned.[18]

Centuries later, the Saviour Himself came to this world and shared the same kind of burden which the prophet bore: "O Jerusalem, Jerusalem, that killeth the prophets, and stoneth them that are sent unto her! how often would I have gathered thy children together, even as a hen gathereth her chickens under her wings, and ye would not! Behold, your house is left unto you desolate. For I say unto you, Ye shall not see me henceforth, till ye shall say, Blessed is he that cometh in the name of the Lord" (Matt. 23:37-39).

In these last days, before the Lord returns, God is still calling modern prophets like Jeremiah to witness to the lost multitudes. And for the judgments which He shall continue to send, individuals and nations alike may learn from this inspired book of Lamentations just how they may find deliverance.

---

[18]No doubt the number of converts was very small. One of the most tragic revelations of Scripture is that most sinners run further away from God when He sends judgment. Read Rev 9:20-21 and 16:21 to see how unbelievers will react to the final judgments of the last days.

APPENDIX I

THE CHRONOLOGY OF JEREMIAH

The book of Jeremiah was written over a period of time spanning the rule of five kings of Judah, from Josiah to Zedekiah (1:2-3). Most of the message has reference, however, to only three of the kings, since theirs were longer and more crucial reigns. The order of the kings was: Josiah (640-609); Jehoahaz (Shallum, 609); Jehoiakim (609-597); Jehoiachin (Jeconiah, 597); Zedekiah (597-586).*

By and large the book of Jeremiah follows a *general* chronological sequence. That the chronology is not always followed is seen in the following example:

21:1, "when king Zedekiah sent unto him"

25:1, "in the fourth year of Jehoiakim"

Are such "dislocations" very frequent in Jeremiah? The following study demonstrates the rather consistent chronology of the book.

From 36:27-32 one learns that part of the total message of Jeremiah was originally incorporated in a "first roll" (v. 28). This could well have included all of chapters 1 through 20. When this "first roll" was burned by King Jehoiakim, Jeremiah had Baruch duplicate this original message, supplementing it with a body of "added . . . words" (v. 32). The sum total of these added words approximated the original roll, if the intent of 36:32*b* is

---

*Dates from John C. Whitcomb's chart "Old Testament Kings and Prophets," Grace Theological Seminary, Winona Lake, Ind.

141

"and there were added besides unto them as many words as they," a possible rendering of the Hebrew text. The sections 25:1—26:24, 35:1—36:32, and 45:1—51:64, dealing with the days of King Jehoiakim, may have been part of the "added words," each section being purposely located in the total book of Jeremiah at a later date. A third part of the total message of Jeremiah was that written during the days of King Zedekiah and after the fall of Jerusalem. Chapter 52, very similar to II Kings 24:18—25:30, is a supplement attached to the end of the book.

The above observations lead to the following scheme of Jeremiah, where it will be seen that a chronology is generally followed within each major division.

Three Main Divisions	During Reigns of
BOOK I 1	Josiah; Jehoiakim mainly (possibly some Josiah sections)
BOOK II (with insertions of "added words") 21	Zedekiah mainly (Jehoiakim insertions: 25, 26, 35, 36)
	Governor Gedaliah
SUPPLEMENTS 45	Jehoiakim; Zedekiah

The chronological pattern of Books I and II is generally in this order: JOSIAH, JEHOIAKIM, ZEDEKIAH, AND POST-ZEDEKIAH. The supplementary section (45-52), included at the end of Jeremiah with purpose, understandably reverts back to the reign of Jehoiakim.

The following is a list of datelines (explicit date references) in Jeremiah:

Josiah: 1:2; 3:6
Jehoahaz: none
Jehoiakim: 22:18; 25:1; 26:1; 35:1; 36:1; 45:1
Jehoiachin: none? (see 22:24, A.S.V., margin)
Zedekiah: 21:1; 24:1,8; 27:1,12; 28:1; 29:3; 32:1; 34:2; 37:1; 38:5; 39:1; 49:34; 51:59

APPENDIX II

CONTEMPORARY KINGS AND WORLD POWERS DURING JEREMIAH'S PROPHETIC CAREER

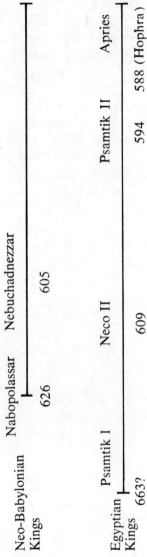

J E R E M I A H   as   PROPHET

627 — c.575

Neo-Babylonian Kings

Nabopolassar 626 — Nebuchadnezzar 605

Egyptian Kings

Psamtik I 663? — Neco II 609 — Psamtik II 594 — Apries 588 (Hophra)

640	609		597	586	
JOSIAH	JEHO-AHAZ	JEHOIAKIM	JEHOI-ACHIN	ZEDEKIAH	

Kings of Judah

640	612	605	597	586	
ASSYRIAN ASCEND-ANCY	Egypt vs. Babylon for Assyrian Control	NEO-BABYLONIAN ASCENDANCY			

"World" Power

Fall of Nineveh

Battle of Carchemish
Nebuchadnezzar's Siege of Jerusalem
70-year captivity begins

Nebuchadnezzar's Second Invasion of Judah

Final Siege of Jerusalem

Fall of Jerusalem

Brief Sketch of the Kings
(see II Kings 22-25; II Chronicles 34-36)

Josiah (640-609). At age 8, he began a reign which lasted for 31 years. Overall, it was a righteous reign with revival activity (temple repaired, Book of Law found, a great Passover kept, and reforms against idols made) beginning in Josiah's twelfth year, one year before Jeremiah began his prophetic ministry. Nineveh, capital of Assyria, fell in 612; the Egyptian armies moved across Palestine, and Josiah, attempting to halt them, was slain at Megiddo, 609 (II Kings 22; 23:1-30; II Chron. 35:20-27).

Jehoahaz (Shallum, 609). The third oldest of Josiah's sons, he was appointed king by the people at age 23, for an evil reign of three months. He was then taken captive to Egypt by Neco, king of Egypt, where he died (II Kings 23:30-34).

Jehoiakim (609-597). Neco II made 25-year-old Eliakim, son of Josiah and elder brother of Jehoahaz, to be king, changing his name to Jehoiakim. He held an evil reign for 11 years (see Jer. 22:13-19; chap. 36), taxing the people and giving tax to Neco. In the third year of Jehoiakim's reign Nebuchadnezzar besieged Jerusalem (Dan. 1:1-2). This was the first deportation, and from this date (606-605) the 70-year exile period began (cf. Jer. 25:11-12). Jehoiakim was taken into servitude by Nebuchadnezzar, whom he served for three years, before rebelling. Soon thereafter, he died or was murdered (II Chron. 36:5-8; II Kings 24:1-7).

146

Jehoiachin (Jeconiah or Coniah, 597). Son and successor of Jehoiakim, his evil reign of 3 months began at age 18. He was taken captive with thousands of others (the second deportation), then released 37 years later (II Kings 24:8-17; 25:27-30; Jer. 52:31-34).

Zedekiah (597-586). Mattaniah, uncle of Jehoiachin, was appointed king over Judah at age 21 by Nebuchadnezzar, who changed his name to Zedekiah. His evil reign lasted 11 years (see especially II Chron. 36:12-16). Though he was a vacillating, indecisive leader, he was not antagonistic toward Jeremiah. Zedekiah made secret alliances with surrounding nations, rebelling against Nebuchadnezzar, who besieged Jerusalem for almost 18 months before finally capturing it. Zedekiah was taken captive with his people in 586.

APPENDIX III

THE GEOGRAPHY OF JEREMIAH

As can be seen by the accompanying map, Palestine ①, Jeremiah's homeland, was the bridge between Egypt ② and the Mesopotamian empires of Assyria and Babylon ③. Though the Israelites had by nature an intense nationalistic loyalty, they were not immune to the foreign viruses which invaded their spirits via commerce, travel, and political aspirations. As a military power, Judah had been made virtually impotent by God because of her sin. Now she found herself being moved back and forth between nations, with each change of world suzerainty.

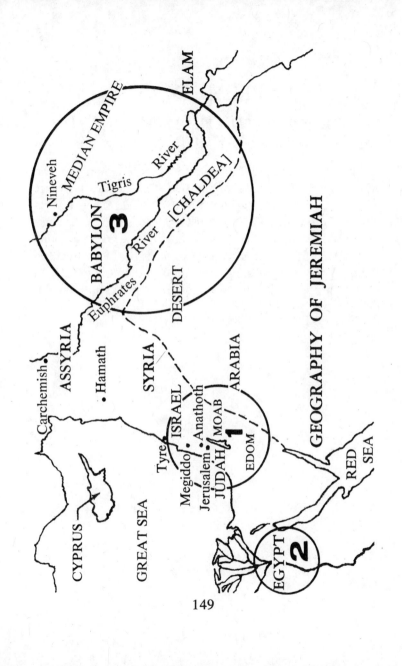

GEOGRAPHY OF JEREMIAH

APPENDIX IV

THE WRITTEN AND LIVING WORD
OF GOD

The Prophecy and Lamentations of Jeremiah are two of the thirty-nine books of the Old Testament. They are part of the infallibly *written* Word of God. They are related also to the *living* Word of God, Jesus Christ, because He is the theme of the Bible's story. The accompanying tabulation of the common characteristics of the written and living Word of God suggests, among other things, that a Christian application of Old Testament books is unavoidable.[1]

[1]Tabulation is by Norman Geisler, *Christ: The Theme of the Bible,* p. 112. Used by permission.

THE WORD OF GOD

Written	Common Characteristics	Living
II Tim. 3:16	Divine Origin	John 1:1
Heb. 1:1	Human Nature	Heb. 2:14
Rom. 3:2	Jewish Mediation	Heb. 7:14
Ps. 119:138	Faithful	Rev. 19:11
John 17:17	True	John 14:6
John 10:35	Without Error (Sin)	Heb. 4:15
Matt. 5:18	Imperishable	Heb. 1:8
I Peter 1:24-25	Unchangeable	Heb. 13:8
Rom. 1:16*	Power of God	I Cor. 1:24
II Peter 1:4	Precious	I Peter 2:7
Heb. 4:12	Sharp Sword	Rev. 19:15
Ps. 119:105	Light	John 8:12
Luke 4:4 (from Deut. 8:3)	Bread	John 6:51
Ps. 119:129	Wonderful	Isa. 9:6
I Cor. 15:2	Saves	Heb. 7:25
I Tim. 4:5	Sanctifies	I Cor. 1:2
I Peter 1:22	Purifies	Titus 2:14
Ps. 119:9	Cleanses	I John 1:7
Ps. 107:20	Heals	Matt. 4:24
I Peter 2:2	Nourishes	John 6:58
John 8:32	Liberates	Gal. 5:1
Ps. 119:50	Makes Alive	John 5:21
I Peter 1:23	Begets Sons	I Peter 1:3
Matt. 5:18	Lives Forever	Rev. 1:18

*Some of these verses refer to the spoken word of God which later became the written Word of God.

BIBLIOGRAPHY

DAVIDSON, FRANCIS (ed.). *The New Bible Commentary.*
Grand Rapids: Wm. B. Eerdmans Publishing Co., 1953.
Short but up-to-date commentaries on Jeremiah and Lamentations included in this one-volume Bible commentary.

HILLERS, DELBERT R. *Lamentations.* Garden City, N.Y.:
Doubleday, 1972.

KEIL, C. F., AND DELITZSCH, F. J. *The Prophecies of Jeremiah,* 2 Vols. Grand Rapids: Wm. B. Eerdmans Publishing Co., 1880. Excellent study of the text; rather
technical.

LAETSCH, THEODORE. *Jeremiah.* St. Louis: Concordia Publishing House, 1952.

LESLIE, ELMER A. *Jeremiah.* New York: Abingdon Press,
1954.

MORGAN, G. CAMPBELL. *Studies in the Prophecy of Jeremiah.*
New York: Fleming H. Revell Co., 1931. Study of the
highlights of the prophecy, written in a nontechnical
style.

PEAKE, A. S. (ed.). *Jeremiah and Lamentations* in The New
Century Bible. Edinburgh: T. C. & C. C. Jack, 1910.

PFEIFFER, CHARLES F., and HARRISON, EVERETT F. (eds.).
The Wycliffe Bible Commentary. Chicago: Moody Press,
1962. Excellent one-volume commentary.

SCHAFF, PHILIP (ed.). *Lange's Commentary on the Holy
Scriptures,* Vol. 6. "Jeremiah" and Lamentations." Grand
Rapids: Zondervan Publishing House, n.d. Excellent
commentary.

SMITH, GEORGE ADAM. *Jeremiah.* (4th ed.) New York:
Harper & Bros., 1940. Revised and enlarged.

VON ORELLI, C. "Jeremiah," *The International Standard Bible Encyclopaedia, III*. Grand Rapids: Wm. B. Eerdmans Publishing Co., 1939, 1588-91.

WHITE, W. W. *Studies in Old Testament Characters*. New York: The International Committee of the YMCA, 1904. Suggestions for studies in Jeremiah.

WOOD, FRED M. *Fire in My Bones*. Nashville: Broadman Press, 1959. Interesting topical style.